A Tale Out Of Season

Dr. E. Mei Shen

Copyright © 2021 by Dr. E. Mei Shen

All rights reserved. No part of this publication may be reproduced, distributed, or transmitted in any form or by any means, including photocopying, recording, or other electronic or mechanical methods, without the prior written permission of the publisher, except in the case brief quotations embodied in critical reviews and other noncommercial uses permitted by copyright law.

ISBN: 978-1-63945-304-7 (Paperback)
         978-1-63945-305-4 (E-book)

The views expressed in this book are solely those of the author and do not necessarily reflect the views of the publisher, and the publisher hereby disclaims any responsibility for them.

Writers'
BRANDING

Writers' Branding
1800-608-6550
www.writersbranding.com
orders@writersbranding.com

The author used fictitious names for many of the prominent characters in this book due to privacy issues.

Dedication

To my husband, Joe, without whom this book
would not be written.
To my children, Angela, Sylvia and Laura.
Your existence has enhanced mine immeasurably.
And to Harriet - "There is no medicine to be found for a
life which has fled."

I sat alone in the library brooding. *What to do…what to do…what to do?* The question swam around my brain. Why couldn't I just decide and be done with it? Did fears of regrets immobilize me? Should I make this critical decision all by myself? What if I didn't make any decision at all?

What a mess. How did my life unravel so fast in just one year? How did I allow myself to get in this position when I had worked so hard to attain my goal? I had barely started to fulfill a promise made to myself when I was less than ten years old in the shadow of death during the Japanese occupation in Shanghai.

I started to review the parts of my life leading up to this point.

Seven years earlier, I had entered the United States as an exchange student to pursue postgraduate training in medicine. I remember it was a Sunday, and it was almost eight in the evening when the train pulled into Lowell, Massachusetts. Earlier, I had landed in New York City and then spent the rest of the day rushing to get on the right train to Boston and then changing trains from Boston to Lowell. I was too tense with worry to appreciate my new surroundings.

Now settled on this last leg of my journey, staring out of the window, I caught my first conscious glimpse of America unfolding before me, a panorama of houses that all appeared to have the same style, packed closely together, built mainly of wood, a distinct contrast to what I had been used to. Where I was from, houses were designed by architects and no one would live in a house resembling their neighbors.

Oblivious to the other passengers on the train but aware of the clanging of the wheels, I reflected on how lucky I am to have achieved my life's goal and to be given the opportunity to expand on that ambition in a country renowned for its achievements in medicine.

The evening dusk gradually descended upon us when we finally arrived in Lowell. I lugged my trunk down from the train onto the platform and entered the station that looked deserted except for a lonely ticket master. He directed me to the public phone. With the right change in my hand, I dialed the hospital number and asked to speak to Dr. Martin.

"I'm sorry," said the operator. "We don't have any Dr. Martin on the staff."

Panic rose, and I said, "But you must. He is the director of the hospital who signed my contract. I am the new intern."

"Oh," she answered. "You mean *Mr.* Martin. He is at home now, and you can reach him with this number."

It was stunning to me that a non-MD could be director of a hospital. I dialed Mr. Martin's number and heard a deep pleasant voice say, "Steve Martin."

"Mr. Martin," I said, "I am your new intern. I have just arrived at the train station, and I would like to know if I should proceed to the hospital."

There was a long pause. "My God, you speak English."

What kind of an idiot is this? I asked myself. *Did he think I would travel some ten thousand miles to treat patients without knowing the language?*

My disrespectful thought was immediately interrupted by, "Wait there. I'll be right down to pick you up."

Mr. Martin soon arrived in his dark green Cadillac with the fins, definitely *the* car to have in the late 50s. As he emerged, I noticed he was a very distinguished-looking handsome gentleman with a head of silvery hair. He looked suspiciously at me as if still unsure whether I had spoken English.

He extended his hand for me to shake it and said, "Steve Martin."

I said, "Thanks for picking me up."

He opened his car trunk and attempted to lift my luggage. When he couldn't do it at first, he asked, "Do you have a dead body in there?" That was my first exposure to a country without a caste system. I would never have expected a director of a hospital to joke with a lowly intern.

I didn't know what to say, so without commenting, I helped him raise my trunk into his car.

On the way to the hospital, we explained to each other what had happened. I explained that I had sent him a telegram to inform him of my arrival. He had not received it and, therefore, was not prepared to house a new intern. Though, he assured me that the housekeeper, Ms.

Alma Galey, would take care of me. When we reached the hospital, Mr. Martin summoned Ms. Galey, a fairly large buxomly, stern-looking, gray-haired woman who also looked at me in a suspicious way, then guided me to a well-furnished room. When she found out that I had not eaten, she promised to try to find some food for me but I don't remember anything more about that night.

The next morning, I woke up with a start, totally disoriented. I found myself fully dressed and lying on top of the bedcovers. Slowly, it seeped into my consciousness. I was in a foreign country. I looked at my watch. Nearly seven. Was this right? Yes, I had adjusted my watch in New York. Thank God for that.

I sprang into action, opened my trunk, and pulled out my "whites" which were badly creased. And since I was unaccustomed to wearing anything creased, I decided to do something about them. I pulled open closet doors until I found an ironing board with an iron and attempted to press out the creases which stubbornly refused to disappear. A little sprinkling of water along the crease would have done the trick, but I had no idea because I have never ironed anything before. My life had been one of privilege, a diplomat's daughter with numerous servants to attend to all my needs.

After fifteen minutes of this futile exercise, I gave up and climbed into my rumpled uniform.

Just as I was ready to leave, I heard a soft knock on the door. It was Ms. Galey who had come to take me to breakfast. She explained that she did bring some food for me the night before, only to find me fast asleep. I thanked her for her kindness and followed her down the stairs and out the door to a beautiful quadrangle, bordered on each side by brick buildings. Flowers bloomed along the base of these buildings, and an American flag flew at the center of the quad. Along the walkway, parallel to the buildings, everyone we met uttered, "Lovely day" or "Beautiful day" or "Great day." I wondered, Why *are they making such a big deal about a sunny day.*

That was before I'd been exposed to New England's weather.

We finally reached the other end of the quad and entered a side door into the cafeteria. Being so late, the place was almost empty. Ms. Galey directed me to the food that was in big metal trays. I decided to have a boiled egg and coffee—safe choices for someone who had no idea what was in a typical American breakfast. To my utter surprise, I was handed the egg in a small saucer. How was I supposed to eat an egg from a saucer? This really puzzled me. I had always had a boiled egg in an egg cup (a small chalice-like devise that holds the egg so it can be tapped and peeled and evacuated by the spoon). I carried my tray to where Ms. Galey sat, and I slowly sipped my coffee so I could think. I looked around to see if anyone was eating an egg like mine but couldn't find anyone. In the meantime, Ms. Galey was watching me intently. I could almost hear what she was thinking. *What's the matter with that girl? When is she going to eat that egg?*

I needed to do something soon. With just a half cup of coffee left, I picked up the egg and tapped it against the tabletop until the shell was shattered all around. I then started to peel the egg. By that time, I was so nervous confronting Ms. Galey's unwavering stare that I dropped the egg into my coffee. With a brave smile, I said "We always do this back home."

I do not remember eating the egg. I walked out of the cafeteria in a bit of a daze and headed for the ward with Ms. Galey, where I was introduced to the head nurse. She was surprised to meet a new intern and, after welcoming me, walked me down the rows of beds, giving me brief sketches of each patient's problems. There were ten beds altogether, five on each side of the room. Retractable curtains separated the beds, and I noted that eight of the beds were occupied by women. I was told that the men had a similar ward across the corridor.

I was also informed that meeting available staff members was next on my itinerary. The first doctor I met was Dr. Benjamin, another distinguished-looking man with gray hair. He was the chief of surgery, and he greeted me with warm words of welcome. In the middle of exchanging pleasantries, he unexpectedly asked, *"Parlez vous francaise?"* I surprised him with a no. He then confessed that it was his opinion that any non-English speaking foreigner who could speak English well could probably speak French too. I was sorry to disappoint him.

After him, I met two other surgeons and an internist. Each welcomed me too and expressed hopes that we would work well together. Last, I met the other intern John Themos, who was toiling away, waiting eagerly for my arrival. He rushed to give me a bear hug—something I was not accustomed to—and said, "Thank God you are here." He looked exhausted, and no wonder. This was a three-hundred-bed hospital, and we were going to be the only interns plus three surgical residents rotating together from the surgical services of Boston City Hospital. They were replaced every four months by another set of three residents.

John did not waste any time in giving me an overall view of our responsibilities. We were both in charge of every patient admitted to the ward, plus any private patient that our assigning staff member wanted to give us. On admission, we were responsible for the clinical history, a preliminary diagnosis, lab tests or x-rays orders, and medications. All of this needed to be dictated as soon as possible so that legible documentation and not scribbled notes would be in the patient's charts. Rounds were to be made each morning on these patients with an assigned staff member. He would discuss the cases with us and help us take care of these patients.

We would be on call every other night. In other words, if I were on call on Monday, I would be working from 8:00 a.m. Monday to 5:00 p.m. Tuesday, covering the whole hospital with the surgical residents. There would always be a staff member on call for help or advice. We would rotate, spending three months in each of four areas of the hospital: medicine, surgery, obstetrics, and pediatrics. When I asked if anyone was in charge of us—that is, monitoring our progress or lack thereof—being that we were interns, I was told that the pathologist, Dr. Dunham, was the man. We would meet with him every Friday for lunch and discussions.

I then learned that John had graduated from Harvard College and went to Greece for his medical degree. Unlike me, he had no previous experience as an intern. I had had a year of internship as a requirement for graduation.

I also learned that John lived within walking distance of the hospital with his new bride and that he took calls from his home. He sounded a little defensive when he mentioned that, and it made me think that to do so was perhaps inappropriate.

Just when I was about to ask him something, I heard my name paged for the out-patient department. John hastily directed me to where that was, and I found myself in a room with a screaming boy. Mother and nurse were both trying to calm him, but he remained kicking and screaming at the top of his voice. He was brought in for a vaccination, but he would not stay still for anyone to do it. I saw Dr. Benjamin passed by, but then he stopped and retraced his steps back into the room. After he learned what was going on, he asked us to leave him with the child. We stepped out, and within a minute, the screaming stopped. Dr. Benjamin beckoned us back to do our job. I vaccinated the boy who surprised us by thanking us.

When I caught up with Dr. Benjamin later, I asked him what he had done to calm the child. He said, "I grabbed him by the collar and told him if he didn't stop screaming and let you do your job, I would come back and knock his teeth out." I thought, *Is he joking?* He didn't look like he was. *What strange people these Americans are.*

After being told by John that I was assigned to medicine, I admitted patients the next few hours. In between I was called to the emergency room and saw a young man with a fishhook through his eyelid. I saw the protruding tip was pronged, so I couldn't pull it out. The other end had a bulb-like feature where the string was attached. I couldn't pull this end out either. I looked at this problem for quite a while and had no idea what to do. The ER nurse approached me and diplomatically asked quietly if I needed help. I nodded. She left the room and came back with one of the surgical residents who was nearby. Dr. Bloom looked at the eyelid and asked, "First time you've seen this?" I nodded, feeling very incompetent. He asked for a wire cutter, snipped one end, and pulled out the hook by the other end. Voila, so that's how it's done.

I had managed to get through the morning without any disaster so it was with great relief that I headed to the cafeteria for lunch this time. I got in the food line and looked at what was offered. I had no idea what I was supposed to do, so I asked for a hot dish and picked up many small dishes, like the one with a square of Jell-O, another with a scoop of some kind of salad, and another that I recognized as egg, plus a cup of coffee. I always had to have coffee. It reminded me of home. Coffee was what got me through medical school. When I dreamed, it was of my mother asking me if I had enough coffee. I moved up to the cashier, who took one look at my tray and said, "My, Doctor, you must have hollow legs." I had no idea what that meant.

I carried my tray to the doctor's dining room and saw all these gentlemen seated around the table, all having soup. Every one of them stared at my tray as I made my way toward Dr. Benjamin, whom I recognized. I sat beside him and acknowledged his introduction of the doctors around the table. Most of them were surprised to know that I was the new intern. All greeted me warmly. While they watched me eat all the food on my tray, I was also watching them and what I saw absolutely floored me.

Dr. Benjamin was bringing a spoonful of soup to his mouth when drops of the soup spilled onto his tie. Without a moment's hesitation, he licked his index finger with spit and then applied the finger to where the soup had dropped. I nearly fell off my seat. Did he, the chief of surgery, just clean his tie with his spit? No one looked perturbed. Did this mean that cleaning spots off your clothes with your spit is the norm here in America? For the second time I thought how strange Americans are.

I was off for the night. The next morning, I met Dr. Roshon, an internist assigned to me for the month. He made rounds on all the patients with me. I found Dr. Roshon a very smart disciplined thinker with a laser beam focus on my diagnoses. He systematically and logically went through with me the reasons why we should keep a diagnosis or discard it for another. His questions were never random and, if answered correctly, usually pointed me to a specific path I should take. This kind of one-to-one teaching relationship was new to me, and I enjoyed it tremendously. He was a very good teacher, and I was an avid learner. I began to look forward every day to his rounds with me and prepared as hard as I could to answer his questions correctly. As the days passed, he appeared to be enjoying the rounds too. Our discussions became more energetic and in-depth. Although there is the usual hierarchal separation between teacher and student, he never behaved like a teacher who was always right. I was learning a tremendous amount of medicine, especially in the area of diagnostic skills. I loved these rounds and tried my best never to disappoint Dr. Roshon. Over time, after our stimulating rounds, we fell into the habit of having a cup of coffee together when time permitted, chatting freely about our backgrounds.

I told him I was born in the Dutch East Indies (Indonesia today) and grew up all over Southeast Asia because my father was a diplomat who was last assigned to the Philippines where I went to medical school and graduated from the University of Santo Tomas in Manila.

He told me that he grew up in China because his parents were missionaries. He impressed me as an unassuming and humble person, so I was not surprised when he lamented that he was of the same age as one of the two Chinese Nobel prize winners in physics for that year, a nugget of information which seemed to belittle his own accomplishments.

I thought it was amazing that he grew up in the land of my ancestors and I was being taught by him in the land of his origin. Although I am Chinese, I had spent most of my life outside of China. The few years that I did live in China was under the Japanese occupation, which almost took my life.

To my dismay, my rotation with Dr. Roshon flew by speedily. I did not want it to end, but it had to. On our last day together, I expressed my heartfelt appreciation for his role in my medical education. I had taken full advantage of his generosity in teaching me all he did. Also, in the entire one-month period, he had scrupulously avoided making me his peon by demanding my service for his private patients.

I was next assigned a general practitioner who did not disguise his disdain for his assignment. We went through rounds like a hurricane, leaving many of my questions hanging in the air. He acted like he really didn't care what I did or didn't do for these patients.

Even worse, he would hand me a list of his patients whom I had to interview and get their admission histories in the chart before the day ended. He was too lazy to do it himself. I was definitely the cheap labor at his command for the month.

Without the help of a staff physician, I came to rely heavily on the nurses who were wonderful, not only to me but also to the patients. They were all older than me, and their attitude towards me was one of intense protection. They shielded me from abuses by the staff, reminding them that I was already overworked. They would gently suggest better plans of action when mine didn't seem quite right. And most of all, on rounds with them every morning, I could trust them to give me detailed reports of every change in every patient under our care.

In addition to their protective care, they tried to acquaint me with "the American way of live." They invited me to their homes for dinner, where I watched with amazement their banters with their children. Again, something strange to me. My relationship with my parents was rather formal. I do not recall ever telling a joke to my father, nor did I ever talk to him about the dreams or ambitions I had for myself. Still, I will always be grateful he never opposed any plans I had for myself and, in fact, supported my endeavors without any complaints, paying the high cost of my education even during difficult financial periods after he resigned from his diplomatic post. Although I was sure that he was quite pleased with my achievements, he never went out of his way to tell me so and I did not think it unusual until I witnessed the intimacy exhibited between parents and children of my hosts. Perhaps it was because I had been taken care of by untold number of servants, from maids to cook, houseboys, gardeners, and chauffeurs. Perhaps I spent too little intimate time with my parents. Perhaps it was just a difference in culture.

At any rate, it surprised me that a simple observation between American parents and children caused me to seriously reflect on my upbringing.

Maria, a staff nurse approached me one day, hoping to expand my education about America, and invited me to go out to a typical American restaurant. This turned out to be Prince Spaghetti located on Washington Street in Boston. She ordered for me so I would be assured of getting a genuine American dish. It came as a big surprise. It was noodles smothered in a red sauce.

How did noodles become American? Ah, Marco Polo, of course. He brought the noodles from China to Italy, and the immigrants brought them here. Definitely a side benefit of immigration.

The meal did not "feel" American to me; so, when Claire, a petite, beautiful staff nurse, said that she would take me to a really authentic American restaurant called Durgin Park, I accepted at once. She drove me there and found their parking lot full, except for a tiny space into which she decided to back in. After repeated tries, she finally managed it and we were greeted with a round of loud applauses from a line of people extending from the restaurant's door. Claire got out of the car and gave a gracious bow to the crowd. She then ushered me to the end of the line.

I asked her if we were getting free food for standing in the line.

She said, "No, the line is a testament to the popularity of the place."

"Do you not have reservations in America?" Obviously not in popular establishments. When we were finally seated at a long table with other diners on a bench, I noticed that the table was covered by a red-checkered tablecloth and the floor was covered with sawdust.

The waitress took our orders and served us roast beef so enormous that it draped over the edges of the plate. The service was accompanied by unending insults throughout the evening like "Picky, picky," when Claire wanted sour cream for her baked potato instead of the butter served. When bringing coffee to our neighbors on the bench, she looked at us and said, "Stop talking. There's a long line of people waiting for you to leave." I took all this to represent authentic American practice. This was definitely an experience which I clearly remember to this day.

The experience of having one plate of food with representations of protein, carbohydrate, and vegetable as a meal always brought back a flood of memories of the sumptuous feasts prepared by the extraordinary chef we had while we were in Calcutta, India. He was a master of western cuisine, having served once as a chef on the Cunard Line, and a wizard at creating the most beautiful and tastiest Chinese dishes. One dish I particularly remembered was in the shape of a lobster featuring a large lobster head with each and every spiny projection on the head topped by a beautiful animal carved from carrots, radishes, and green melons. The body was made up of a collection of fried shrimp balls, and the whole dish was completed by an authentic lobster tail. Our chef was so secretive about his recipes that he would not allow any of us into the kitchen when preparing for a feast. He had his own assistant who came to help him. This same assistant would show up to cook our dinner because it was too boring for our chef to cook a simple dinner.

The Calcutta assignment of my father was a terrific showcase for this chef's talent. Calcutta between the years 1942 to 1947 (when we were there) was considered an important post for China. Any VIP, including Madame Chiang, who, on leaving Chungking (China's wartime capital), flew over the Himalayas and landed in Calcutta for a stopover. Moreover, those years were turbulent years for India: the Muslims were fighting the Hindus and both were fighting the British. The fighting actually extended to the streets of Calcutta. To curb the violence, curfews from ten in the evening to six in the morning were put in place by the British military, accompanied by warnings that anyone seen on the street within these hours would be shot. A little old English lady decided to challenge this by walking her dog after ten. She firmly believed that no British soldier would ever shoot anyone English. She was wrong. She was shot, and that execution was advertised widely to convince everyone that the curfews were serious orders, enforced without exceptions. Cars on the street, during the day, belonging to white nationals other than English, were draped with flags of their respective country to prevent being mistaken for being English and thus killed by the Indians. We were escorted daily to school by an armed guard.

To remain relevant in international relations, China indulged the post and—incidentally, us— by allowing us to have a maharajah's palace as our residence, replete with marble floors and banisters (a wonderful slide for us when no one was looking) complemented by tinted light green windows wrapped around the entire upper floor of twenty or more rooms. The diplomatic corps in Calcutta was a very active group, meeting constantly for dinners to discuss international affairs. My parents were hosts three to four times a week, filling our dining room with distinguished guests. The dining room had an alcove closed off by a curtain through which my siblings and I would often peek to catch a glimpse of the diners, the most prominent of which was Mr. Nehru. Although Mr. Gandhi was never one of the diners, my father did spend two weeks with him at his mountain retreat. I remember my father remarking when he returned from the visit that he smelled like a goat. This was due to the heavy dose of goat products in their daily diet.

When World War II ended, the five victors over Japan, which included China, gave spectacular victory parties to celebrate the event. I remember our party because my mother was worried about the amount of liquor my father was going to take in the form of toasts from the guests. She diligently instructed the houseboy how he should substitute tea for the whiskey when serving my father. This scheme failed miserably when most of the guests demanded to toast my father with mao dai, a colorless potent Chinese rice wine. He was soon toasted under the table.

The party had an atmosphere of pure joy with total abandonment of proper diplomatic decorum. Cheers were yelled, laughter roared. For one night, it seemed, memories of the misery of war were left behind. The event lasted through the night, and when we woke up in the morning, we found guests in our bathtubs, in our garden, and under bushes.

Calcutta, in my memory, is the dirtiest city I have lived in. Busy thoroughfares always showed men washing themselves at the fire hydrants while other men dotted the pavement with their backs against buildings, eating their food with their fingers. "Sacred" cows strolled leisurely along the streets, depositing collections of dung in their pathways. Occasionally one would decide to sprawl and rest in the middle of the street. Woe to drivers encountering one of these sacred animals blocking traffic without the slightest fear of being towed away. I recall one such incident where horns were blasting away trying to prod the animal to move without any success. Instead, out of boredom, we moved out of our car and discovered vendors selling delicious hot, spicy fried beans and nuts in paper cones. An instance of pleasure in the midst of chaos.

In 1947 my father was transferred to Manila, Philippines, in time for the new nation's inauguration of their first president, Manuel Roxas. My father asked our chef to go with us, but he politely declined because he felt the rate of entertainment would not be enough for him to show-off his talents. We learned that he left us to become the chef of T. V. Soong, Madame Chiang's brother, who was representing the government in Washington, D. C.

Life in the Philippines during my teenage period left indelible impressions.

The Philippine Islands, having been a colony of Spain for many centuries, shows a heavy Spanish influence in all things Filipino, most notably in the area of religion, evidenced by a population of devout Catholics. Not being one when I entered a Catholic school, I was generously exempted from taking the course on religion. Since this was a rarity in that school, this exclusion made me conspicuous among my fellow students. I will never forget the shock I received when, seated on a swing with a classmate, she said to me, "You're not a Catholic. Did you know only Catholics go to heaven?" Religion up to that time had been a minor element in my life despite the fact that my maternal grandfather was a Methodist bishop who spent seven years on Hainan Island translating the Bible into vernacular Chinese. I had a general sense that good people went to heaven and bad ones went to hell, but I certainly did not know that only Catholics went to heaven. It was the start of my antagonism toward religion.

It was also in the Philippines that I experienced the first sting of discrimination. The Chinese population in the Philippines was a minority group, but they dominated the commercial landscape, creating, over time, considerable resentment by both the government and the populace, resulting in unfavorable laws passed targeting Chinese. Daily petty exchanges between the races were a constant reminder of the discord. One such event which I remember, illustrating this tension, was during the Asian Games where the Chinese basketball team (from Taiwan) played against the Filipinos for the championship in Manila. When the Chinese team was ahead near the end of the game, spectators started throwing things onto the court. A bottle hit the star of the Chinese team in the head, resulting in a big gash. The mayor of Manila, who was present at the game, got onto the floor and pleaded with the spectators to stop, without success. The Chinese team withdrew immediately, enabling the Filipino team to be champions by default. In the aftermath of this debacle, it was discovered that the Chinese team was mainly made up of players who lived in the Philippines. The Taiwan government acknowledged that fact and claimed that they recruited those players to save their government some money. The end result of an event founded for the promotion of international goodwill resulted in legislators proposing laws not only prohibiting Chinese in the Philippines to play for Taiwan but also to disallow them to play on teams in the Philippines.

In medical school, after the first year, students were divided into "upper bracket" from the rest based on grades and you had to maintain a certain grade to remain in the "upper bracket." The school took this designated better group of students seriously and gave them the best teachers, providing them with a very good medical education. I managed to be in the upper bracket throughout my medical school years, and yet when I asked for my transcript during my internship in the US, I was surprised to find that I was officially ranked "in the middle" on my transcript.

Still, I remember life in general was pleasant. I have lifelong friends among my classmates with whom I recall fondly of enjoying lunch breaks in the little food stores behind the school, eating pancit (noodles), roasted pork with their delicious sauce, and the small concave shaped rice cakes as desserts.

I also now have nephew and nieces who are Filipinos. They remind me of all the good things in the Philippines.

Back to my life in Lowell, extra examples of Americana offered by my friends included a visit to a not-so-up-and-up nightclub called the Blue Moon in Lowell, where I first tasted a concoction called a screwdriver and an invitation to a fifty-yard line seat at a Harvard-Yale football game, which was definitely an eye-opener for me. Expecting to see a soccer game (called football around the world), I was thoroughly confused by the powwow of the players, the throwing of the ball, and the chasing of the man carrying the ball who was attacked with such ferocity when caught. The only connection I saw between foot and ball was when the ball was kicked over a bar, known as the goalpost.

Harvard won the game, and while we walked across the bridge to Harvard Square, I witnessed swarms of grown men waving little flags with an *H* on them and singing at the top of their voices. Since I laughed and looked puzzled, my host gave me a short history of the rivalry between Harvard and Yale, thus explaining the bizarre behavior.

During this period, when I was trying to absorb as fast as I could all things American, I was being subjected to what I termed *Americanese*. For instance, I was told not to discuss anything with one particular person because she was a *fruitcake*. This same person was referred to as *batty*. When a nurse committed an error, she was *toast*. These strange terms mystified me. It became serious when a young boy came in one day to the ER. When I asked him what was wrong, he said, "Charley horse."

I replied, "You are Charlie, and you own a horse."

"No, no, I *have* a charley horse."

It took an interpreter to tell me that charley horse meant cramps.

My experience in the ER, where I met people with all kinds of background, brought out an interesting fact. They all appeared surprised and downright uncomfortable when I appeared as the doctor. I was definitely an oddity. I could almost hear them collectively thinking, *she can't be a doctor. She must be a nurse.*

Even though some of these patients showed an obvious preference for a male doctor, it was to their credit that none refused my treatment.

I did not blame them. After all, the entire hospital medical staff had just *one* female physician. She was elderly, rarely seen, and was referred to as a "kook" because she was often seen talking to herself. I was never introduced to her, and she appeared unaware that I existed.

My last month in medicine was spent with another general practitioner who was a little better than the last but still fell far short of my expectations. I was eager to move on into surgery. When I did, I fell under the tutelage of not only the staff surgeons but also the surgical residents from Boston City Hospital. The surgical residents were unique and wonderful to me. The oldest of the three was a handsome Italian bachelor who played the guitar beautifully. Every student nurse was out to get his attention. The second was an Irishman; and the third, a Jew. Within a short while, all three of them decided they could trust me with their patients and allowed me to be on call for them while they went on dates. They would leave with the standard warning that I not call them except in extreme circumstances. For these favors, I was rewarded the next day with surgical tasks that no interns were allowed. I loved this arrangement and was eager to be in their good graces.

One morning, I met Gary, the Irishman, on my way to the cafeteria. I had been on call for him the night before.

He greeted me with, "You missed a fracture last night."

"I did? How did you find out?"

He answered, "I just came from the X-ray department reviewing last night's films with the chief."

Oh God, I thought. *How did I do that?* My face must have reflected my distress because the next thing I knew, he had his arm around me, grinning, "Don't feel so bad. The chief missed it too. I spotted it only because I had a case just like this. It was in the patella. Very hard to see. Go look at the film again. You won't miss it the next time."

Rounds with them were not only learning experiences but also amusing. I had a patient who reminded me every morning to never ever be an internist if I wanted to avoid all kinds of neurotics. She was in for some minor surgery but was kept in the hospital because of her unending complaints that drove me crazy trying to sort them out. I had her last on my list each morning.

This morning I had Gary with me to help me out. As we both stood beside her bed listening to her litany of aches and pains, starting from her head meandering down to her toes, Gary interrupted her and asked, "Tell me something. Do you have an itch behind your eyeballs?"

She eagerly answered in the affirmative and added, "No one here is helping me."

Gary then solemnly assured her that he knew what was wrong with her and would take care of her problems. Out of earshot from the patient, Gary said to me, "Anytime a patient tells you the back of her eyeball itches is the time you label that patient a nut. Get a psychiatric consult and send her home." I have never forgotten this. There are times when I am tempted to ask some of my friends the same question.

Almost half a year into my internship, I was sleeping an average of four hours a night, which never changed throughout the year. Because I lived in the hospital and the other intern John Themos did not, I was very often called even though I was not on call for the night. ER nurses would apologize profusely and complain to me that when Themos was called, his wife would answer the phone with the only sentence she knew in English, "Dr. Themos is not at home." I did not mind the extra calls. Even on my weekends off, I would be asked to assist surgeons who either couldn't or didn't want to get an assistant. On one such assistance, we were operating on a child with an intestinal hernia. Just as the operation was ending, the surgeon nicked her small bowel and had to spend extra time repairing it. I wondered how the surgeon was going to explain this to the parents. I never did find out. What I did find out, to my horror, was that the surgeon blamed me for the incident.

Stephano, the senior resident, was so incensed when I told him about this that he went to Dr. Benjamin on my behalf to complain about that surgeon. This resulted in a total change of behavior from all the surgeons. I was no longer asked to do things to benefit their private practice giving me some much desired breaks, but despite these changes, there never seemed to be enough time to do everything on time. Themos and I often met to complain about the workload. So together we decided to complain officially to the hospital director, Mr. Martin. To our surprise, he agreed with us and promised that he would try to get another intern to help us out.

This new intern turned out to be a man from Turkey, who was supposed to be a chest surgeon. He arrived answering most of our questions with a yes and thank you. Because we were so stressed out, we decided to put him on call right away. On that very night, he appeared in the ER in his pajamas, trying to treat a person with a heart attack. It became quite evident then that *yes* and *thank you* were the only English words that he knew. The nurses went berserk and staged a revolt, refusing him access to patients. I was called to fill in for the night. The administration could not boot him out since he had a contract for a year, so they made him an X-ray orderly, wheeling patients to and from X-ray and taught him how to say "Take a deep breath."

So much for the extra help Themos and I got.

As my rotation in surgery was coming to an end, Mark Bloom, the junior resident asked me one day what I wanted to do after my internship. I told him that I really enjoyed surgery and that I wanted to be a gynecological surgeon, which would require training in general surgery. He agreed that I would be good at surgery and surprised me by volunteering to make an appointment for me with his chief of surgery at Boston City Hospital. Mark drove me to the hospital and introduced me to his chief, saying a lot of nice things about me. The chief was a very kind gentleman who interviewed me and emphasized to me the difficulty of a surgical program. First, I would have to start at the bottom, meaning another year of surgical internship. Then I would have to compete in a pyramid system where residents were eliminated at the end of each year for four successive years going into the fifth year. A resident eliminated in the second or third year, would find it difficult to get into another good surgical program to continue on. He also gently reminded me that surgery was a very tough residency where you are on call every other day for five straight years.

I thanked him for his time and gave his advice careful thought.

To specialize in gynecological surgery, I would need at least two years of general surgery and then two or three more years of OB-GYN training. I finally decided that I should try to get into an OB-GYN program first. I applied to all the existing programs in Boston and several outside of Massachusetts. I was rejected from all because I was not a US graduate and/or because there were no facilities to accommodate women on call.

By now I was through with my obstetrics rotation, which was an easy one compared to my previous experience in the Philippines. There, I was placed in a government hospital where everyone seeking admission was accepted. After delivery, the patient was put in any space that was available, often on the floor in between beds, and I had to go around waking up strangers to identify my patients so I could hand them over to the next shift.

When I was assigned a difficult case that needed a Caesarian section, I was responsible for getting the blood typed for possible blood transfusion. If needed, I was expected to go to the blood bank away from the hospital to get the blood. The on-call period was exhausting, and it was the only rotation in our internship where we had a whole day off following a twenty-four-hour duty.

I was now three-fourth of the way through my internship, and I needed to enter into a residency program to renew my visa to remain in the country. This is where Dr. Dunham, our mentor and the hospital's pathologist, came to my rescue. Themos and I met with him every Friday. He critiqued our work and informed us of any staff member's complaints about us. In addition, he listened to our complaints and we learned a bit about the pathology of the patients in our care. Patients who were autopsied were studied during these sessions. Here, I must have shown more than an inkling of interest because Dr. Dunham started to invite me to autopsies of private patients and soon permitted me to actually perform the autopsies under his supervision. What I found fascinating in an autopsy is that each case represented a mystery for me to unravel. Since I am an aficionado of mystery novels, I relished the challenge. I fancied myself a detective, diligently matching the abnormal anatomical findings in an autopsy with the clinical signs and symptoms during life, discovering at times totally unsuspected disorders, rivaling the obvious cause of death. These postmortem examinations were exciting and worthwhile.

I am sure that I was the only rotating intern in the country who did about twenty autopsies during an internship. Dr. Dunham also invited me to his home on weekends and on holidays like Thanksgiving. He had a lovely wife and three gifted children, the oldest of whom could read and write six languages including Hebrew at the age of fourteen. They lived beside the famous Phillips Academy known around the world as Andover, where his oldest child attended. It was on one of these weekends that he asked me what my plans were at the end of the year.

I told him my depressing story and expressed my reservations about going into a surgical program. He agreed and suggested that I should take a year of pathology on the basis that a good foundation in pathology is never wasted no matter what specialty I decided to enter. I couldn't disagree with that philosophy so he said he would immediately inquire about a residency at the hospital where he had had his own training. A day later, he informed me that all the positions were filled but he would try something else.

A week later, Dr. Colle, chief of the department of medicine at the hospital, called me to confirm my interest in a residency in pathology. He told me he was a personal friend of the pathologist-in-chief at the Medical Center and that he would be happy to go to see Dr. Mann in Boston on my behalf. I was astounded that Dr. Colle would do this for me though I hardly knew him. I thanked him profusely and expressed my deep appreciation.

Soon after, I received information and application forms from the medical center about their program. It informed me that the first year of residency was not at the medical center but at an affiliated community hospital. If the candidate's performance was satisfactory, then she/he would then move on to the medical center for the next two years.

The first year represented an introduction to the usual kind of pathology found at a community hospital while the years at the medical center would introduce the trainees to the unusual kind of pathology found mostly in specialized centers. I was accepted into the program and assigned to Mount Auburn Hospital located in Cambridge, Massachusetts. I was very happy about that and relieved that my residency in America was assured for another year.

My year at Lowell drew to a close with my final assignment in pediatrics. There I learned that I could never be a pediatrician. I did not like to hear children cry.

In a year I had made many friends, particularly student nurses who were closer to me in age than the staff nurses. One of them was Barbara, a hardworking, independent, and smart woman who had befriended me. She would take me home with her on the weekends where I met her mother. I learned from Barbara that she earned her way through school by working weekends and holidays at a small private hospital near her home. Up to that point I had not known anyone who worked to put themselves through school. I couldn't imagine myself doing it, and so I was filled with admiration for her. She continued pursuing her educational goals up to postgraduate level and became a much-respected teacher. We remain friends until she passed away this year.

While I was still in Lowell, I had dinner at the elegant Vesper Country Club via the generosity of a surgeon and attended a much-appreciated steak dinner for interns and residents given by a well-known drug company. The affair was very subdued. There were no introductions of the drug company officials. There were no speeches. No samples of their products were handed out. None of us felt any sense of guilt eating those wonderful steaks.

The practice of feeding poor interns once a year by drug companies came to an end several years later due to the intense rally by physicians to stop this practice, which was interpreted as a payola of sorts. Gifts to interns in the form of stethoscope, otoscopes, and medical bags were also discontinued based on the same principle. To deprive poor interns from these wonderful and useful gifts unfortunately did not deter physicians from practicing a more direct form of payola from pharmaceutical and medical device companies to "push" their products.

My year finally ended. Many of the physicians rewarded me with books inscribed with their appreciation for my help. I really did not want to leave. The workload had been hard, but I loved it and found it exhilarating despite the fact that when I sat down and calculated the pay I received for my labor, I found I had earned a grand sum of twenty-two cents an hour for the year.

Mount Auburn Hospital is located in Cambridge and is well-known as a teaching hospital. It is mainly affiliated with the Harvard training programs, but trainees from the other medical center were also present from which I was a representative.

My first day at the hospital was a blur. I was introduced to my fellow trainees: Bernardo from Chile, a studious-looking young man with a twinkle in his eyes as he greeted me with a slightly exaggerated manner, and Alicia from Mozambique, who was pleasingly plump and very suave with a unique accent.

Dr. Mann, chairman of the department of pathology at the medical center and titular head at Mount Auburn, and Charles, the working chief of pathology at Mount Auburn, with his associate Tina, completed the makeup of the team.

The specialty of pathology consists of two main divisions: anatomic pathology (AP) and clinical pathology (CP). One could be in a combined residency or separately in one of the two. The medical center had only a residency program in anatomic pathology so that was what we were in. In this branch of pathology, there are two main areas of interest: surgical pathology and autopsy pathology. They are commonly referred to as surgicals and posts (for postmortem examination).

Soon after the formalities, Tina met with all of us. She assigned me to surgicals with Alicia as my backup and Bernado to autopsy. She then explained what was involved when we were on surgicals.

Surgical specimens were delivered to our surgical "cutting room" all day long from the operating room. We needed to label all the specimens received with numbers in an ascending order. The same numbers were also given to the OR (operating room) slips attached to the specimens, which contained patient information, diagnosis, and the items submitted.

Next, we needed to dictate the gross appearance of the specimens, take representative sections to show the abnormalities, and place them in metal cassettes to be labeled with the corresponding surgical numbers. These cassettes were then to be placed into a container filled with formalin, a fixative used commonly for tissues.

At the end of the day, this container needed to be hooked onto a special machine that dipped the cassettes in different fixatives in timed periods throughout the night. In the morning, the histology techs would remove the tissues from these cassettes to "block" them in paraffin, which allowed them to be cut by a microtome, producing tissue sections that are microns in thickness. Strips of these cut tissue were then floated on a bed of warm water from which a blank slide coated with a sticking gel would be positioned under the strip to pick up the desired tissue sections within the strip. These slides, properly numbered again, would be placed in a slide tray that would then be dipped by hand into various containers of dyes to stain the tissues. Once this is done, each slide would be covered with a glass coverslip and put into a special slide file, ten on each side, to be delivered to us for review and diagnosis, usually in the early afternoon.

It was our job after our dictation to go over these slides, write down the microscopic descriptions, give a reasonable diagnosis, and have everything ready to be reviewed with Tina or Charles in the morning. Alicia as my backup would review the slides with me.

Tina was a very good teacher. When the diagnosis was wrong, she would patiently point out what I had missed and offered suggestions as to how I should go about reading a slide in an organized manner. Differential diagnoses were discussed and subtle changes from one cellular characteristic to another were often shown and stressed. Patterns of certain disorders needed to be learned and memorized. That was the easy part. The most difficult part to making a correct diagnosis was the ability to detect the earliest subtle change from normal to abnormal. Acquiring that ability meant a thorough mastery of what is normal in all its variations.

Tina was not only a patient teacher she turned out to be a wonderful "guardian" to us. She would invite us to her place for dinner, would accompany us to the famous Boston Pops, would give us solid personal advice for personal problems, and would even lend us money when we needed it. Tina was not her name. She became Tina because back at home she had a maid named Tina whom she missed a great deal and talked about her incessantly when she first came to the US. Her friends started to tease her by calling her Tina and the name stuck.

While learning has its own pleasures, learning to describe something in a concise and precise manner took time. It was not enough to state, "There is a tumor in the segment of colon removed," I needed to learn how to measure the length, the width, and the depth of the tumor; to state how far it extended through the wall of the colon; to describe the tumor's shape and consistency, whether it was hard, soft, or necrotic; and how far it was from the margins of resection.

Then I had to learn to be accurate in taking the appropriate sections to show the abnormalities. Everything in the beginning appeared to take forever. Charles, whom we renamed Carlitos, when compared to Tina, was a hopeless teacher. I once asked him why he thought it was diagnosis A and not B, and his answer went like this, "You know Tina, right? If she happened to be walking in front of you and you only saw her back and not her face, you would still know it's Tina, right?"

I answered, "Yes."

He said, "There you are."

Carlitos had other flaws in his logic. He could not distinguish between what was anti-American policy discussions from being anti-American. This posed problems for us because we often discussed American policies that were not helpful to some parts of the world and Carlitos would interpret these chats as anti-American He hated foreigners, and he had the bad luck of having three of us under his tutelage. We avoided him as much as possible, and he pretended we were not his residents.

Soon after we settled in, Bernado, Alicia, and I received invitations to Dr. Mann's annual bash for all his trainees, a tradition that is carried out yearly by all department chiefs in a show of collegiality.

Dr. Mann lived in an exclusive area in Cambridge, in an elegant house nestled along Brattle Street. It was an impressive abode. So, while I was seated on his comfortable sofa, eyeing the crowd, he approached me to ask how I was getting on and how were my accommodations at the hospital.

Thinking that his inquiries were sincere, I started to tell him my sad tale of woe: My room was a converted storeroom so small that I could not turn between my bed and the bureau. My bed sagged so much that I had to put my trunk under it to support it. The parked cars came right up to my window so that the shades had to be drawn at all times. And my room was decorated by a hanging hot water pipe, dangling from the ceiling, transforming my room into a sauna, the heat of which could not be relieved by opening the door because the male residents had to pass my room to get to theirs. I understood that this was not the usual fare because the hospital was in the process of building a new dorm for their resident staff. But surely, I thought, things could be a little better.

Almost immediately, I realized that I had made a dreadful mistake. He smiled, looked elsewhere, and left me before I'd finished my first sentence.

What I truly did not understand then was the prevailing sentiment toward residents. We were just cheap labor, and the attitude was, "Take what we give you and please don't complain." The appalling living conditions, however, did imbue in me a lifelong habit of never leaving beds undone nor allowing objects to be strewn about to mar the orderliness of a room.

I was clearly miserable. I also had a lot of free time compared to my time as an intern. Back then, I had always been busy, always needed and known by everyone in the hospital. Here, aside from Bernardo, Alicia, and Tina for occasional company, no one else was friendly. Residents from other specialties did not seek us out because, from their viewpoint, anyone who aspires to be a pathologist was one who was generally odd, antisocial, and obviously someone not suited to taking care of living patients.

To battle my loneliness, I explored Harvard Square in my free time, the long lines of stores, and the famous newspaper stand located on an island of space between the university and its flagship store the Coop. I even explored the university. When Harvard was first pointed out to me, I almost cried. I had envisioned it to be in the likeness of Boston College with cathedral-like buildings and tree-lined pathways, not as a collection of brick buildings between patches of grass. This disappointment did not deter me though from taking oodles of photos of John Harvard's statue sitting serenely in front of his building with me beside him for my friends back home who were in awe of anything and everything Harvard.

The Harvard Book Store became my favorite haunt. It was on one of my visits that I ran into a classmate. Both of us were flabbergasted when we found that we were within walking distance of each other. She and another classmate were in an anesthesia residency at the Cambridge City Hospital. She immediately invited me to have dinner with them. While there, I was amazed to find out that they had never eaten a single meal at the hospital's cafeteria, preferring to cook all their meals in their bedroom on a hot plate.

They didn't have any American friends, and they had not explored any parts of Cambridge nor Boston. Although I visited them often, ate food with them often, I could not persuade them to go anywhere with me. Not to the Pops, not to the Esplanade to hear the Pops, not to a single interesting place.

The local medical profession generally did not embrace foreign medical graduates, mainly because of our inability to express ourselves well in English. This furthered an impression that we were not as well educated as their American counterpart. Because of these prejudices, foreign physicians tended to keep to themselves and complain incessantly about the unfair treatment they endured.

Since I spoke English well and without an accent, I was usually mistaken for an American school graduate and was not subjected to any discrimination. For that reason, I stayed clear of any collections of foreign medical graduates. When my friends in Cambridge ended their residencies a year later, they took a trip across America in a Greyhound bus before heading for home. It was definitely not my idea of learning about America, but their action fitted their temperament. For me, I was deeply grateful for their presence in Cambridge and for brightening my life immensely.

Back at work, I continued to creep upward along a steep learning curve but not without a few hiccups. On my watch, one day, an irate surgeon stomped into the department and charged us with losing an appendix he had removed with another specimen the day before. Tina calmly assured him that we would find it. When he left, she asked me to go through the trash. I went through three bins of bloody, stinky material before I found the appendix still wrapped neatly in a piece of gauze. I suddenly recalled the case. The main specimen was a uterus submitted in a container with mounds of gauze. I had simply gathered up all the pieces of gauze and chucked it. I couldn't believe that I was so sloppy. Not only had I not checked each piece of gauze, I had not read carefully the OR slip on which the appendix was clearly listed. I had to tolerate a bit of snickering from Bernardo and Alicia, but it was a lesson well learned. I moved on to be assigned to autopsies.

A teaching hospital is required to autopsy 20 to 25 percent of the deceased in order to keep its residency program. The true rate then was close to 40 to 45 percent of all deaths. Getting permission for posts was never an easy task, one which usually fell on the shoulders of interns who took care of the patient. Among the many reasons families refused autopsies, the most illogical one was, "He/she has suffered enough."

Thankfully, most relatives were reasonable and could be persuaded, especially when told that the cause of death needed to be confirmed by the postmortem examination.

Dr. Mann, who was a stickler on how an autopsy should be done properly, took upon himself to instruct every one of his residents on their first autopsy. Since I already had about twenty autopsies under my belt, I thought this was going to be a breeze.

I was dead wrong. The first thing I was told was that he did not want to see any blood—not on the body, not on my gloves, not on me. If it was on the body, I was told to sponge it away. If it was on my gloves, rinse them. If it was on my apron, change it.

After reciting to him the clinical history of the deceased, we proceeded to the first incision. He instructed me how to assess the organs *in situ*, how to remove each organ and weigh each one, how to section each part removed, and how to meticulously examine each section for abnormalities. The scalp was incised in a special way, and the skull entered into through two specific cuts, and the brain removed without squashing it. At the end of this six-hour lesson, after many changes of my apron, he made me summarize what I had observed, system by system, starting with the cardiovascular, followed by the pulmonary, gastrointestinal, renal, genitourinary, endocrine, and, finally, the cerebrovascular system. We then discussed what provisional diagnosis we should submit, and instructions were given to me as to how it should be written. The probable cause of death was to be placed at the top, followed by contributory causes, followed by incidental findings. This report was to be sent immediately to the attending doctor, who may wish to call the relatives to discuss the findings. A final report would be submitted when the microscopic examination of all the organs was completed.

I was exhausted. Dr. Mann on the other hand looked fresh and relaxed, despite the fact that he was at least thirty-five years older than me. This is the man who was once asked to perform an autopsy clad in a tuxedo, ready to go to a formal party. He did it in his tuxedo, finishing with nary a drop of anything on himself, then left for the party.

He was trained in Germany, and his demands on us to have all autopsies performed in the absence of the usual blood and gore reflected his own training. It also indoctrinated all of us to a lifelong practice of countermanding all the perceptions held by the general public and propagated by imaginative novelists about autopsies.

After Dr. Mann's first tutorial, Tina supervised all other autopsies and was just as rigorous. After all, he trained her. Similar to my stint on surgicals, my rotation in autopsy did not glide along without a disaster. I was doing a postmortem examination of a case of probable perforation of the colon following a long history of diverticulitis. The presence of perforation was immediately evident upon the initial incision due to the fecal odor and the extensive amount of pus covering the organs. The task for me here was to locate the site of the perforation. For that, I decided to remove the gastrointestinal tract *in toto* and laid it aside for a more careful scrutiny. I finished my examination of the rest of the body and had the body removed so that I could have the entire table for my task, aided by a steady stream of water squirting out of the nozzles from the sides of the table and a vacuum system at the end of the table sucking up all the undesirable material from the GI tract.

I separated the stomach and small bowel from the large bowel, the latter being my area of interest, and focused my attention on a line of saclike out- pouchings called diverticula along the borders of the colon. I was very excited to find the exact point of the perforation and the cause of it—a small triangular fragment of what appears to be a part of a crab or lobster shell lodged within the perforated diverticulum. So intense was my focus that I was startled by the sound of the door latch, admitting Tina into the room. Turning my head, I lifted my hands and before either of us could say, "Oh my God," the vacuum gobbled up the entire GI tract. As I stood stunned and motionless, Tina dashed to the end of the table and turned off the vacuum.

A jumble of thoughts ran through my head. *I'm going to be drummed out of this program. How am I going to explain this to Dr. Mann who surely would be informed of this colossal error? What am I going to say to the surgeon who happened to be the same guy who justly accused me of losing his appendix only a month ago?*

My rambling thoughts were sharply interrupted by the urgency in Tina's voice. She said, "Let's see if we can retrieve this."

The first thing we did was to push a wire into the vacuum to see if we could reach the bowel and therefore ascertain that it was still within the reservoir and had not been sucked into oblivion. We confirmed its presence. Next, we bent the end of the wire into a hook to try to pull the specimen back. This effort was totally unsuccessful. Finally, the *diener* (a term meaning "helper" in German) suggested that we call the Roto-rooter man. I thought he was joking, but on second thought, the idea did not sound that outlandish. Tina agreed. We told the diener to call and ask for someone who would not faint at the sight of human parts. The story ended happily, enabling me to continue my training.

Aside from my periodic stumbles, I was progressing satisfactorily. I also slowly developed a strong liking for the thoughtful and solitary aspect of this specialty and decided that I should stay with it, prodding myself to work harder.

To be a good pathologist, I felt required certain qualities. One is a good eye to detect the subtle cellular changes. Others include the ability to enjoy working alone, a love to solve mysteries, and to possess a nature that is happy to exult privately in one's achievements unaccompanied by public praise. No patient will ever say to a pathologist, "Thank you, Doctor, for saving my life because you made the correct diagnosis." Others will happily take that credit. Patients, even today, have a very vague impression of what a pathologist is and what they do and what part they play in their health care despite the few TV series highlighting the specialty in a skewed way.

During our training, Bernardo, Alicia, and I had become friends and we managed somehow to go to lunch together on most days. We had decided early on that we would not discuss anything medical during this break. Since the two of them were rather cosmopolitan and educated in the arts, we would spend the lunchtime discussing Ingmar Bergman's films, Nabokov's novels, or the differences in our cultures. On occasion, we would talk about politics, mainly American policies and its impact upon the world. Soon, other physicians began to join our table, energizing our discussions. At times, the conversations became so intense that we would be followed back to our department to achieve a conclusion. Carlitos, being there, would feel obliged to add his two cents worth. Invariably, he would leave in disgust. Had he had the power, he would have thrown us out of the department on the claim that we were all communists.

My year did not end without a memorable and disagreeable staff encounter.

Mount Auburn Hospital had many distinguished physicians on its staff. Among the best known were Dr. Harten, a heart surgeon who was a pioneer in the repair of the mitral valve of the heart, and Dr. Saachi, our chief radiologist, whose name was in every textbook that had a chapter on esophagus.

One morning, I was up for the next post and that happened to be on a man who died suddenly the night before when under the care of Dr. Harten's associates. Dr. Harten was not pleased. I was informed that he would be at the autopsy. Dr. Saachi too was going to be present because his department had performed several procedures on the deceased, and he was eager to find the cause of death.

I had already reviewed the clinical history and so was ready to proceed in the presence of these two distinguished doctors.

As soon as I exposed the chest cavity, we all knew why he died. The sac holding the heart was filled with blood. The aorta and the carotid arteries were swollen with blood within the walls, diagnostic of a dissecting aneurysm, a condition caused by a tear in an artery allowing blood to seep into the wall. In this particular case, the aorta was torn, allowing blood to flow into its wall and into the walls of the carotid arteries arising from the aorta.

I stopped to get my camera to take photographs of the findings, a task imperative in a teaching hospital where mandatory mortality conference was held monthly to discuss in detail all cases ending in death, accompanied by photographic support of the gross and microscopic findings. As I stepped off the stool, I heard Dr, Harten scream at the top of his voice, "Goddamn it, I didn't ask for this post for you to take pictures." I was instantly paralyzed into inaction while curses rained on me.

From the corner of my eye, I saw Dr. Saachi leave the room and the next thing I saw was Tina walking in and taking over. She suited herself up, calmly picked up the camera to snap several shots, and took over where I left off with the autopsy. Close to tears, I quickly left the room. On my way back to the department, I bumped into the chief tech of the blood bank. Noting my distress, she asked what was wrong. I told her, and she said, "He's a jerk. Every time his patient dies, he storms into the blood bank and accuses me of killing his patient. Don't pay any attention to him." She patted me on the back and left.

That afternoon, the chief of surgery came into the department looking for me. When he saw me sorting out the surgical specimens, he put his arm around me and said, "I heard Dwight misbehaved today. He is not a bad man, and I am sure he will come by to apologize to you." I nodded, fearful of bursting into tears. He also patted me on the back and left.

Dr. Harten never did apologize, and my esteem for him, which was pretty high before the incident, sank to zero. A week later, I witnessed him tearing into a fellow (one doing a fellowship) in radiology who was presenting a case at a surgical conference.

Sean, the fellow, was not that forgiving. On a day, when Dr. Harten had a patient on the operating table, Sean gowned up, went into the operating room, stood behind Dr. Harten, and said in a voice loud enough to be heard by everyone, "Killing another one of your patients?" Sean was from Ireland.

By this time of the year, Dr. Mann informed me that I had made the grade to continue my training at the medical center. Alicia left to pursue her interest in cytopathology, and Bernardo decided to continue his training in radiology, also at the same medical center.

I have always harbored a suspicion that Dr. Mann accepted me because of Tina. She was an outstanding resident under him, and he may have thought that I might perhaps reach her level of excellence. After all, we did graduate from the same medical school. Whatever his reasons, I was thrilled. Before leaving, I had an added task of taking a new examination required for foreign graduates to make sure they were qualified for training in the US. This test was put in place a year after my entry into the US. The ECFMG (Educational Council for Foreign Medical Graduates) exam evolved into a visa requirement to enter the US for postgraduate medical training.

I proceeded to move onward and upward across the Charles River to Boston. The change of venue was jarring. For the first time, board and lodging were not included in my stipend of $350 less taxes per month to meet all my needs. In addition to myself, I now owned a car, a Saab, that I had to support. My Saab was a 2-cycle engine car that propelled itself on the same principle as a lawn mower and, like a lawn mower, had to be fed both gasoline and oil into the same tank. I christened my little white car Lolita. A VW beetle was what I really wanted, but I didn't want to spend an extra five hundred dollars for it.

Bernado had taught me how to drive with a manual shift in his VW beetle in and around Boston. When I thought I was ready and went to take my driving test, the officer examining me addressed me politely as "Doctor" and directed me through heavy traffic.

I was driving up an incline when he asked me to stop halfway up. I did, and as I changed gears to advance, my car slipped back an inch. He immediately asked me to stop and said "That's it, miss." He got out of the car and failed me on the spot. No "Doctor" for me this time. Such is the price of failure. The second time I took the test, Bernado kept the officer so busy chatting with him that I could have gone through a red light and still passed.

My home became a room in a basement, one in a row set aside for women, in a medical student's dorm across from the medical center. The cost of the room and lunches eaten at the hospital were tallied and subtracted from my stipend each month. I soon realized that deficit spending would be on the horizon if I didn't do something to supplement my income. Luckily for me, Bernardo, who was in the same situation, was more creative. He had found a job covering nights in the emergency room of a small hospital north of Boston. Since he couldn't cover seven nights a week without totally destroying his social life, he sought me out to divide the coverage between us. Having had two years of internship, I thought I was qualified and so accepted his proposal. It was a godsend.

At the medical center I was one of two females on the resident staff and the only foreigner. I was also the youngest. I was always the youngest in my peer group. This was due to the Second World War and to the fact that I had managed to leapfrog through the different educational system in the different countries I lived in.

Whenever my father was transferred to a new country, I would be asked by the new school to take an examination for placement in the proper grade. These placements always resulted in one or two grades higher than the one I was in before. These unusual circumstances allowed me to finish elementary and high school in six years, graduating at fifteen, finishing college at eighteen, and medical school at twenty-three. Although I have noticed signs of admiration from friends for this particular fact, the truth is that I have always been conscious of my own huge gaps in knowledge in myriad subjects, often exposing and embarrassing me when least expected.

Still, I was thankful that at age twenty-six, I had already two years of internship and starting my second year of residency when most Americans were just finishing medical school.

The pathology department I was in now had five residents which included two surgical residents rotating through pathology for six months enabling them to study slides relevant for their surgical board examination and to help in autopsies they were interested in.

Again, for the pathology residents, our main duties were divided between surgicals and autopsies.

The staff pathologists consisted of Dr. Mann, chairman of the department and professor of pathology at the medical school. He was in charge of reviewing our autopsies. Zach, his associate, was in charge of teaching us, surgicals. A third pathologist, Margaret, was part of the department. But she was rarely seen except at the medical school.

Dan and I were assigned to surgicals. Piles of specimens were already evident on a nearby table, neatly numbered. Unlike my previous experience, we now had the luxury of a technician who did nothing but help us with our task. Also, unlike my previous experience, the specimens present were very different. Appendices, gall bladders, skin biopsies, and uteri were not the majority of what was on the table. Instead, what we saw were complicated masses of bowel, breasts, gangrenous legs, spleens, and partial stomachs. Instantly I realized that I needed to hone my skills further in areas relating to the normal anatomy of many of these unusual specimens and to speed up my pace. If not, I would be spending my nights here.

Between us, we decided that one of us would do dictation while the other would take care of surgical duties. I volunteered to dictate first. Despite the help I got from the tech, my first dictation lasted five hours, partly because of the large numbers of specimens and partly because I needed constant advice from Zack as to where I should take sections from many of the cases.

The next morning, I shared with Dan the job of running to and from the operating room (OR), fetching specimens for frozen-section examination, and returning with a diagnosis for the surgeons.

A frozen section is a procedure requested by surgeons when confirmation is needed for a clinical diagnosis for them to proceed as planned or when faced with uncertainties, as for example, finding an abnormal mass unexpectedly, where its benign or malignant nature needed to be ascertained for the surgeon to continue in the right direction.

As the name implies, a piece of tissue sampled from the patient is frozen by a freezing agent then cut by a special gadget called a cryostat. The cut tissue is then placed on a glass slide, stained, and diagnosed microscopically, all within a matter of minutes.

However, Dr. Mann introduced us to a different method which he devised during the war due to the lack of freezing agents. He would teach us to slice by hand the piece of tissue under examination with a very sharp and thin razor blade. A glass slide was pressed on the tissue, and with the razor blade parallel to the slide, the tissue was sliced. The sliced tissue, stuck to the underside of this slide, would then be patted with a pre-stained slide to stain it, after which, any excess stain seen on the tissue would be squirted away with a few drops of water. Last, a coverslip would be placed over the stained tissue and the whole slide placed under the lens of a microscope to be diagnosed. This was the only method used in this department.

While we realized the success of this technique rested on how thin the tissue was sliced, we also realized that these cuts by hand could not possibly match the cryostat's ability to produce tissue slices microns in thickness. Besides trying to learn the tricky technique of cutting the tissue without cutting our fingers, we also needed to learn to adjust ourselves to the distorted patterns produced by the thickness of the cut specimen. Herculean efforts were made on our part to attempt to make an accurate assessment from such distortions.

Little by little, I got the hang of it and the slices got thinner and thinner so that rendering a provisional diagnosis gradually fell into the realm of possibility. Mastering this technique strangely gave me a feeling of accomplishment. A fast rule in the department about frozen sections was that it had to be checked by a staff pathologist before delivery to the surgeon.

During the first few months, afternoons were filled with anxiety studying the slides, the number usually corresponding to the complexity of the case and each case seemed to be more complicated than the last. The textbook of surgical pathology became our constant companion, glued next to our microscopes, teaching us new diagnostic patterns. Dan, if dictating for the day, would join me in reading the slides later in the day. Together, we struggled to manage the workload.

Dan was a better prepared resident. He was actually a practicing pathologist in a rural hospital before he decided to reenter a training program. He had a large family who depended on him for support, so with some basic pathology training, he bravely went out and practiced and made enough money to help out his family, allowing him to resume his interrupted residency.

Despite his experience, he usually stayed longer and appeared to be still at his microscope when I showed up in the morning. He was a big help in getting me through each day, especially on the days when I had to leave to get to my second job.

Dan was a handsome fellow, soft-spoken and gentle. Like Zack, he was very proud of his Italian ancestry, so much so that he would mess up his life by driving a totally unreliable Italian sports car, a Spider, which periodically refused to start. To make sure that he got to the hospital on time each morning, he would park his car at the top of a hill, any hill, using the downhill roll to start the car. There were no hills around the hospital, so very often getting home required fellow residents to give him a push.

Zack, on the other hand, was a dapper middle-aged man with elegant old-fashion manners, and like Tina, he was also a great teacher. Consulting a textbook was one thing we automatically did, but getting an experienced perspective and a strictly systematic and logical approach to the interpretation of the disorders we were dealing with was priceless to me. He was an excellent surgical pathologist and a very kind man who sincerely cared about our welfare. Periodically, he would ask us how we were managing with our meager stipend, and when he found out how strapped we were financially, he would send us to perform paid autopsies for pathologists who were on vacation. The only flaw I could detect in his character was his paranoia toward the rest of the medical staff, a common affliction among pathologists.

Zack also took any complaints directed at the department as a personal affront. Notwithstanding his elegant manners, he was very feisty in his defense of the department, of his residents, of his techs, and of his chief, Dr. Mann. Watching him during those moments made me admire him more.

Dr. Mann, on the other hand, was distant and detached from all things unrelated to pathology. His habit of appearing a few minutes before twelve o'clock noon on Saturdays to start reviewing autopsies drove most of us nuts. Noon was the time we got off for the weekend when we were not on call, and his appearance drew an uncommon amount of under-the-breath curses accompanied by collective groans.

Even though my contact with other staff members of the hospital was limited, I managed to learn that there were three other Chinese on the staff. A neurosurgeon, a famous infectious disease doctor, and a microbiologist. To my surprise, I was approached one day by the infectious disease doctor who invited me and the microbiologist to his home for dinner. There, in a very nice Tudor-styled home in Newton, we had a wonderful dinner. After which, a child was summoned to play his violin for us. This small boy of seven or eight years came into the room with his pants zipper at half-mast and mucus dripping from his nose, which his mother helped get rid of. He gave us a little bow and proceeded to play the *Ave Maria*. It was so stunningly beautiful that I had trouble assigning this unbelievable talent to such a small body. Today, he is a famous world-class violinist.

I also remember one other staff member. He was a famous expert on lipids, who escaped from Nazi Germany. He was a tall, white-haired, forbidding-looking gentleman who commanded respect just by his physical bearing. He did not know who I was until his wife died and I autopsied her.

He requested a special meeting with me to go over my findings. He listened to my detailed report calmly and thanked me at the end. From that day on, he accorded me the extraordinary gesture of always greeting me warmly wherever we were. I was told later by a fellow German resident that he had refused to speak German after he left Germany, but on his death bed after a stroke, he could only speak German and he (the resident) was the interpreter for him until he died.

Charles, our third resident, who was first assigned to autopsies, was forced into pathology for a year because he couldn't wake up early enough each morning to make rounds with the chief of medicine while he was an intern in the department of medicine. Never mind that he would spend entire nights tending to the very sick or that he was one of the best interns on the service, evidenced by the glowing recommendation received by our department from the chief of infectious disease, well-known as the toughest doctor to work under and satisfy. The chief of medicine, however, was totally immune to Charles's humane qualities. He was unwilling to tolerate Charles's tardy habits and so refused to appoint him to a well-deserved first year residency in medicine for the following year.

Charles was a handsome, lanky, suave, witty, laid-back Harvard Medical School graduate. His presentations of his autopsy findings were always delightful, and his interpretations imaginative and innovative. Even when he was very wrong, we were entertained. I always looked forward to these amusing sessions. Charles's wit was not limited to the autopsy suite. He once went to fetch a specimen for frozen section and was asked by the chief surgical resident who knew him very well during his internship, "Are you the pathologist?" He answered, "No. I am just the janitor here to mop up the floor."

Soon, I was appointed an assistant instructor in pathology at the medical school, expanding my horizon. This involved teaching second year medical students basic pathology, two hours, twice a week. My job was to circulate around a roomful of students all peering down their microscopes, trying to focus on what they need to see, with me as their proctor verifying or correcting their identified field or object.

Although this seemed to be a menial job, it enhanced my ability to interact with students who were uniformly all doubting Thomases. These were clever Thomases, and I enjoyed dueling with them.

As my life began to appear more orderly and manageable from the daily duties, to the night job, to the teaching load, I started to take time to make new friends.

One of the first was an American-born Chinese named Lila who was an intern at the children's hospital that was part of the medical center but was operated separately as an individual entity. We met one rainy day in the student dorm where she was looking for a student and I was heading to my basement room to prepare for the flood that occurred each time it rained. She introduced herself, followed me to my room, and helped me move everything off the floor onto my bed. She also told me that she lived next to the hospital and invited me to her home for dinner. I accepted her invitation eagerly, grateful for such generosity, and happily met her older sister, brother, and delightful mother that evening. Her mother spoke very little English, and I could not speak their Cantonese dialect, but we managed to understand each other through gestures and Lila's interpretation. In the days ahead, whenever I showed up at their house, she would say "eat" and start to cook for me if no ready-made food was available. She was like a mother to me.

Lila was the youngest of seven children. Her parents were immigrants. Her father was a laundryman, and life had not been easy. Her oldest sister would tell me many times how she had sacrificed her own education to take care of her siblings when their father died.

Lila had an older brother who wanted to be a doctor. He was admitted to McGill University Medical School in Canada but not to Harvard Medical School, where he was determined to go. Snubbed by Harvard, he decided to change career and became a well-known marine biologist at Woods Hole. When Lila decided to become a doctor, she wanted badly to remain at Boston University, where she obtained her undergraduate degree to attend medical school there. But despite her Phi Beta Kappa credentials, BU did not accept her. She did not want to apply to Harvard because an acceptance there would be a tremendous blow to her brother's ego, so she applied to the only other medical school in town and was accepted. The policy of this school then was to admit one female and one minority student for each year. Since she was both, this gave the school the happy opportunity to accept another male applicant. She would regale me with stories of her unique status as the only woman in her class surrounded by admiring males. One such story involved her anatomy class where her classmates attached strings to all the male cadaver's genitals, which would mysteriously rise whenever she passed by.

Her Boston accent constantly confused me, like "Could you bring the toona up?" Not tuna but tuner. When we visited her sister in Detroit, people actually asked her to say, "Park my car at the Harvard Yard."

I learned that when she was depressed, she would go to shoe stores and try on shoes after shoes. When she thought I was depressed, she would drag me down to Filene's Basement, where she once worked, and we would pick through the piles of clothing items, pulling out things we would like to buy but thought it was still too expensive. She would take these items and hide them in certain places where shoppers would not notice, and we would wait for the price to drop, which they did on a daily basis. Then we'd go back to retrieve them, buying them at ridiculously low prices.

In our spare time, we conspired to "fix up" Dan with a lovely Italian resident in medicine, whom we knew, because I told Lila that Dan seemed to be stuck to his microscope, working all the time.

She was a wonderful friend, smart, thoughtful, and full of laughter.

In time, she would distinguish herself by becoming the first female chief resident in pediatrics in that institution. More than just social friends, our professional paths began to cross more and more. I developed an intense interest in pediatric pathology, which allowed me to garner all the postmortem examinations of children from her institution. Since many of the deaths were due to congenital heart disease, I would be invited to the pediatric cardiology conferences to correlate my anatomical findings with their live cinematic dye studies as it flowed through the hearts. At times, I even made rounds with Lila and her crew, an oddity not accustomed to by clinicians. I became very chummy with the pediatric staff; and they, in turn, regarded me as one of their own. The proof of this relationship was displayed one Saturday morning when I was examining a one-year-old baby who died suddenly. In the process, I happened to nick my glove, witnessed by several residents, including the chief resident who took care of the child. After the post, I dashed off to Boothbay, Maine, with Bernardo and friends to do some snorkeling. Unbeknownst to me, the chief resident suddenly took ill and rapidly went into shock due to septicemia.

The cause was traced to a needle prick he sustained while treating the baby whom I had just autopsied. The residents immediately recalled that I had nicked my glove and may be in the same dire situation. Frantic calls were made to Lila who had no idea where I was. Residents in my own department were called. Dr. Mann was contacted. The police was also consulted but claimed that not much could be done if my whereabouts were unknown.

I returned late Sunday evening to the immense relief of all my friends. Lila told me later that she envisioned me dying somewhere alone.

I had been very lucky. The chief resident was ill for a very long time but did eventually recover. Dr. Mann was not amused. In fact, he displayed an unmistakable disapproval of my unique relationship with the pediatricians. Lila and I became the best of friends, a friendship that I thought would last forever. But that was not to be. Toward the end of my second year at the medical center, her mother fell ill. I heard that she was in another hospital, and I planned to visit her one evening. I was late leaving that day as I ran across the street to the florist to order flowers for her. On my way to my car, I bumped into a medical resident who was presenting a case the next day and asked if I could go over the pathology of the case with him. I could not refuse. When that was done, it was too late to visit Lila's mom. The next day, I was heartbroken to find out that Lila's mom had died the night before. Worse, I also discovered that the florist had failed to send the flowers. I was never able to tell Lila what had happened because I feared that it would sound self-serving and, worse, false. Lila, I think, never forgave me for action that seemed unforgivable.

Despite the fact that she was my maid of honor and that her brother gave me away at my wedding, our friendship tapered to an end.

When the tally of regrets in life is recorded, this one will surely be near the top.

My interest in pediatric pathology continued, and my plans began to focus on obtaining more training in that area. I applied to the famous Children's Hospital around town and was accepted as chief resident in pathology. That was a great relief because board and lodging would be part of the appointment.

With that out of way, in an early part of a new year, I concentrated on finishing my senior residency with a bang. And that's what I did.

Added to my assignments that year was supervising the junior residents and medical students with special projects. Arthur was assigned to me for a month-long project to try to extract chromosomes from blood cells. It involved a tedious process of taking certain blood cells from whole blood, culturing them, and stopping the cell growth at a certain point in their life cycle, then harvesting the chromosomes within the cells. These chromosomes were then photographed so that each pair could be cut out and arranged to set a pattern. Since each step in the process offered possible failures, a lot of blood was needed. Arthur suggested that we extract each other's blood every other day, and I agreed.

Arthur was progressing nicely, managing to record a few pairs of chromosomes. He was recounting his methodology to me one day while reaching for a hypodermic needle from a pile he collected for our use and proceeded to insert it into me. What he did not notice, because he was talking to me, was that the seal around the cap of the needle had been broken. Someone had used the needle and threw it right back into the pile.

I woke up the next day with pain and a mean red streak starting from the needle entry up my arm. I was also burning with fever. There was no doubt I had a whopping case of phlebitis with probable sepsis manifested by the fever. I was admitted to the hospital with immediate round-the-clock intravenous antibiotics. Arthur came to see me every day, pale as a ghost, fearing the worst. He could not forgive himself for the accident. After a week, I left the hospital but additional physical therapy was required to stretch out my arm that stayed bent due to pain. Arthur finished his project with the use of his blood only. He refused to stick someone else. Many, many years later, I heard from a classmate of his that he had become a psychiatrist.

The remaining few months of my residency was spent catching up. All the autopsies needed to be completed and signed out; thus, many of my hours became tethered to Dr. Mann. During these hours, very little conversation took place about anything other than the cases in question.

One case caught Dr. Mann's attention. It was a case of an unusual esophageal-tracheal abnormality presented as an abnormal open tract connecting the two structures. This abnormality caused food taken orally to go into the lungs, which produced the pneumonia that caused the infant's death. When we completed the sign out and being cognizant that I was interested in pediatric cases, Dr. Mann suggested that I write this case up and to submit it for possible publication.

Buoyed by his confidence in me, I worked feverishly to get this done, drawing the defect in multidimensional views for a better understanding of it and thoroughly researching the statistics of this abnormality to emphasize its rarity. I finally finished my short treatise, polishing it over and over before handing it to Dr. Mann for his approval. When I did that, he read my paper carefully and said to me, "Let me tell you a story, Tina." (I was Tina to him for two full years until my last day at the medical center when he miraculously addressed me by own name). "There were these two fishermen who wanted to sell their day's catch at the pier. One made a sign, which said, 'We sell fish here.' The other looked at it and said, 'We don't need the word *we* because no one else is selling fish. We also don't need the word *here* because it's evident that we are selling it here and not there, and we really don't need the word *sell* either because we're not giving it away.' After hearing all this, the other man said, 'Well, we certainly don't need the word *fish* then because everyone can smell it half a mile away.'"

I took a deep breath and was really miffed by his critique of my work. So pretending that I was unaffected by this brutal put-down, I retrieved my article from him and threw it in the trash bin outside his office. This rejection was painful but soon forgotten, and we continued with our sign-outs.

What I learned repeatedly from him was his superb ability to tie everything together in the end in an orderly fashion. A lot of whys were asked, foremost was, "Why did the patient die? If no obvious pathology was present to explain, we asked, "What was the supporting evidence for a probable cause of death? What clinical symptoms matched our pathological findings, and conversely, what did we find pathologically that the clinicians missed in the care of his patient?"

The last paragraph of every one of our autopsy report was a brief clinico- pathologic correlation (CPC) of the case. Learning to write the CPC well required a sharp ability to find the buried clues, ferreting them out much like a mystery novelist seeking specific evidence to solve a puzzle. I will always be grateful to Dr. Mann for teaching me this art.

To accelerate my catch-up, I decided to come in earlier each morning to finish my workload and every morning I was greeted by the presence of Dan in his chair peering down his microscope. One morning, coming in earlier than usual, I saw Dan stretching in his seat with his hands laced behind his head. I noticed a ring on his finger and asked jokingly, "Did you get married last night?"

"I did," he answered.

I was stunned. This was the guy I thought was working himself to death when all the while he was courting after work an Italian hematologist two floors down. I remembered then that I was also really taken aback when I was told that this soft-spoken, gentle person was once a Yale All-American football star. He was just full of surprises.

I congratulated him of course, then laughed heartily when I found out later from someone who was at his wedding that after the ceremonies were over, he couldn't start his car and it had to be pushed for them to make their getaway. Such was life in the fast lane.

April was on the horizon. I had only three more months to go before I start on a new path. I was very excited about going to this prestigious hospital and working under very famous pathologists. Dr. Mann and Zack were both happy for me and urged me to keep in touch.

But my bubble of excitement was pricked when I received a letter in early May from Dr. Volker, the working pathologist at Children's Hospital, welcoming me to the department of pathology as a fellow. I didn't mind being on a fellowship, but fellowships did not include board and lodging, and I really needed that to make ends meet.

I dashed off a letter to Dr. Volker inquiring whether a mistake had been made regarding my appointment. I told him that I had accepted the position of chief resident offered to me by the pathologist-in-chief, Dr. Farmer.

Two weeks later, a reply came from Dr. Farmer, this time stating that I was being appointed as a fellow. I needed to confirm my acceptance as soon as possible. We were already in late May, and I knew I could not possibly get another appointment in two months' time. July is the month when all internships and residencies start in the US and Canada. To stay another year in the US depended on having a job. Reluctantly, I wrote to accept the fellowship. This did not make me feel good about the place where I was going to train in for the next year.

When I finally walked through the hallways of this famous institution and into the department of pathology, I was crushed by disappointment. There were nine of us: one American and eight from eight different countries. There were two fellows, one chief resident, five residents, and one intern. There were not enough microscopes for everyone, and the ones I saw were in such poor condition that I wouldn't attempt to use them for diagnostic purposes. One of the microscopes actually had the base made by one company and the top made by another. Luckily, I owned a microscope and didn't need to share a dilapidated one with someone else.

In addition to the trainees, there were four employees: one secretary, one diener, and two (mother and daughter) histology technicians besides Dr. Volker. The department was too small for all of us, and I felt we were on top of each other. Dr. Volker, the working pathologist, (as opposed to the pathologist-in-chief, Dr. Farmer, who did not work in the department) was too busy to meet all of us together; so, the chief resident met us all and gave us some vague instructions.

There was a general acceptance that the more experienced ones would supervise the inexperienced ones. With that, pairs were made up for the daily surgicals and autopsies. We were informed that on-call duties ended at 8:00 p.m. every day mainly because the fixative machine had to be switched on at that time. Also, any autopsy requested at that hour might last until midnight, not because a new resident might be slow but because hospital researchers could demand all sorts of investigations and sampling of tissues.

With this loose framework, I was asked to do an autopsy the next day because the junior member was ill. It was a case of an unusual congenital heart disease. As I approached the autopsy table to start, I paused to rearrange the instruments on a side table to suit my needs and was startled to hear the diener say, "We do it this way at Harvard," as he proceeded to put the instruments back in their original positions.

"Really?" I said as pleasantly as I could manage. "I'm not aware that autopsy instruments needed to be arranged in a set way."

He didn't answer back, and I decided not to challenge him, knowing that carrying it further was not a good way to start a working relationship. He assisted me ably but went out of his way to let me know that he knew a lot about pediatric pathology. We finished the post amiably without additional disagreements.

As the days passed, it became evident that I did not have much to do other than to review slides of diseases that I was interested in. There were too many of us for the daily chores, and it was almost impossible to get Dr. Volker's attention for any one-to-one type of meaningful exchange.

Dr. Volker, I came to realize, was a genius in pediatrics pathology. He was so above us on so many levels that any exchange of views about pathology must have been laughable and painful for him to endure. He was a Quaker, soft-spoken and extremely kind. I surmised that he must have been in the Navy at one time because his daily garb was always a light-blue shirt, a dark- blue tie seen at times tied inside out, dark navy-blue pants, and a navy-blue raincoat. He was always the first in the department and the last one to leave. He did all the work, all the surgicals and all the frozen sections, and reviewed all the posts. Yet every formal pathology report emanating from the department bore the signature of Dr. Farmer's (the chief pathologist) above that of Dr. Volker's.

Dr. Farmer was a world-renown pathologist. His reputation was earned from his many professional accomplishments, not only in pathology but also in other fields, notably as a pioneer in the use of chemicals in the treatment of childhood leukemia. For many years, however, his main job was that of an administrator of an entity devoted to raising funds for and overseeing cancer research and treatment. He was never seen in the department, much less reading slides or reviewing posts. Residents who wanted to see him needed to make an appointment. Why he wanted to project the illusion that he was part of everything done in the department was beyond me.

I never understood why Dr. Volker tolerated this kind of dishonesty, giving readers of the pathology reports a false impression that Dr. Farmer had a premier role in that report. I realized too, in time, many oddities existed in this department.

For one, many of the residents in the department had appointments handed out to them by Dr. Farmer when he visited the countries of these appointees. This, I found out was the reason why I didn't get my original appointment. Alkam, the present chief resident, was offered the same position a year ago by Dr. Volker; but Dr. Farmer gave that position to an Indian pathologist whom he visited without informing Dr. Volker. When Dr. Volker found this out, he promised Alkam that he (Alkam) would be the chief resident the following year. But before that happened, Dr. Farmer appointed me as the next chief resident. Dr. Volker then had no choice but to deny me my rightful position to keep his promise to Alkam. He simply could not break his promise twice to the same person.

My guess was that, being a Quaker, denying me my rightful appointment must have been a difficult decision for him. After I spent a few months of self-propelled activities, I decided that I should pursue something educationally productive for six months. Cytogenetics was the rage then and Children's Hospital had a top-notch department in that specialty. But I needed Dr. Volker's permission to do this.

Luckily, a unique opportunity arose for me to present my request when I was asked to review some surgical slides with him. I accepted eagerly and prepared conscientiously for the expected interchange of views. There was none.

He read the slides in the manner befitting a genius forced to work with useless people. I sat beside him, silently watching his elbow periodically parked on the slides besides his microscope. These newly cover-slipped slides with glue still fresh around the edges would stick to his sleeve so that when he lifted his arm, the slides would fall off, and it was obviously my job to catch them. I realized at that time that that was perhaps the only reason why he needed someone to sign out surgicals with him.

I did not allow any slide to fall and shatter on the floor; thus, I became convinced that he would surely reward me with a few minutes of his time for this singular achievement. He did, graciously.

I told him I wanted to spend six months of my fellowship studying cytogenetics. He nodded and told me he would arrange an interview for me with the chief. I had not expected such a kind reception to my idea, and I was relieved he hadn't rebuffed me.

I went to the interview, very hopeful that I would be accepted, but I was very wrong. The chief of cytogenetics did not want me to pollute his all- American team. He made it clear that I was not up to the standards of his team because I was a foreign medical graduate and that even if he accepted me, he doubted I possessed the know-how to keep up. I left the interview thoroughly deflated, but before I could report back to Dr. Volker, I was summoned by Dr. Farmer, whose secretary waved me toward where he was.

As I sat in Dr. Farmer's splendid office, in a Harvard-labeled chair in front of him, he informed me that he heard I was interested in cytogenetics and that I should not have had to go beyond the department for that experience since his staff included cytogenetics specialists. Better still, he went on to say, he would like to suggest that I spend six months doing research on Hodgkin's disease.

I had no interest in that subject, but I knew that he was. I was also fairly certain that if I followed his suggestion, the research would morph into a nice paper for him. I knew how this game was played. Back at the medical center, I had heard rumors of a famous hematologist stealing his own fellow's research material and publishing it as his own. Dr. Farmer interrupted my unkind thoughts by asking if I planned to remain in the US. The question floored me. Before I could answer, I heard Dr. Farmer say that he had a lot of influence with the US Immigration Department.

To this day, I am unsure whether he was trying to bribe me or to threaten me. At any rate, I resolved right then that I was not going to do research on Hodgkin's disease. Exiting the building I was just in, I saw Dr. Volker walking toward me. As we walked together, I updated him, telling him about Dr. Farmer's suggestion. He stopped in his track, looked at me over the top of his spectacle, and said, "You did expect that, didn't you?"

I had not, and I certainly did not expect such a stunningly revealing sarcastic remark about our revered leader from him. This struck such a discordant note with me that it jolted me into understanding the depth of discontent in which Dr. Volker rendered his services to Dr. Farmer.

Devoid of a project of my choice, I nevertheless tried to learn as much as I could. Luckily, a neurologist who wanted to spend a year studying children's brains appeared on our staff. He was an excellent teacher who took over the supervision of our brain-cutting session each week. In a very innovative and clinically-oriented way, he would make us trace every insult to the brain down through the nerve tracts to corresponding symptoms. These exercises not only taught us the anatomical connections from brain to nerves but also a wealth of clinical manifestations. During one of these exercises, the neurologist lamented that the brains we were studying were not attached to the spinal cords that contained the nerve bundles connected to the brain and to the peripheral nerves. He stated that the presence of the spinal cord would make our study more complete and would further our understanding of neuropathology. He immediately added that he had never seen a newborn baby brain removed with the spinal cord attached, and he did not expect to see one here simply because it was too difficult a procedure for most pathologist to undertake, considering the fact that the consistency of a newborn brain is much like that of mashed potatoes.

After the conference, Guillermo, a senior resident, approached me and said, "Why don't we do it?" I looked at him and saw that he, being a determined neuropathologist, was not going to allow this challenge go to waste. I nodded in agreement and said, "Let's"

The very next post assigned to Guillermo was a sudden infant death case, and he and I went to work. After we examined all the organs except for the brain and spinal cord, Guillermo and I paused to plan our next move. We knew we had to expose the spinal cord from inside the body, but the instrument used to cut into the bones was too large to use on this infant's vertebral bodies. We decided to chisel the bones along the sides of the entire vertebral bodies little by little in order to lift the bony structure to expose the spinal cord.

We then entered the cranium, cutting through the fibrous tissue in between bones not yet fused into a single bony container of the brain, freeing the brain from its attachments to the pituitary gland, optic nerves, and nerves alongside the midbrain. We then left the brain in its place and went back to the spinal cord to uncover it from its fibrous covering and to sever all the attached peripheral nerves, enabling us to lift the cord free from its bony bed. The final step was the most difficult and our success or failure depended heavily on this delicate maneuver. Guillermo volunteered me for this. I had to hold the brain and tug at the spinal cord to pull it through the opening at the base of the skull. I positioned Guillermo to support the spinal cord as I pulled on it.

Before I began, I had a large jar of formalin ready where the brain would be immersed for fixation.

The cord is a much firmer structure compared to the brain so that indentations by our fingers were less likely to occur and damage it. The brain is covered by the thinnest possible transparent membrane designed to contain it in infancy as a mass. Any focal pressure on it would result in permanent indentations, not ideal for study or investigative purposes. For those reasons, I decided to slip my hands under the brain, gradually lifting it and at the same time tugging it little by little backward using only my palms. After what seemed to be forever and with Guillermo's help, the entire specimen of brain and spinal cord attached was successfully removed from the body and gently lowered into the fixative.

Guillermo and I breathed a celebratory sigh of relief. Added to our self-congratulatory feelings were soft applauses coming from several of the residents who had been watching us for more than an hour. Effusive praise was showered upon us at our next meeting with the neurologist when we presented to him the brain with the attached spinal cord. He could not believe that we had done something so difficult so well. His lecture with demonstration using the infant's brain and spinal cord was magnificent.

By word of mouth, these conferences became so popular that residents from neurology soon joined us. For me, these were the week's best moments.

About this time, I thought I should get to know the residents better. They were from such diverse backgrounds.

Guillermo, for instance was a major in the Mexican army. The speed in which he learned English was astounding. When he first arrived, he could hardly speak a sentence but within months, he was able to converse and joke in the language even though he occasionally missed some subtle meanings, like the time when McDougal, the American resident, told us a story about a man who was bent over, hanging onto a lamppost on Longwood Avenue, the street in front of the hospital, which was bordered by Peter Bent Brigham Hospital and the Women's Hospital. A taxi driver stopped upon seeing this man who appeared to be distressed. Knowing he couldn't take him to either the Children's Hospital or to the Women's Hospital, he yelled, "Peter Bent?"

"No, zipper stuck," the man answered.

While I roared with laughter, McDougal winked and said to me, "Explain it to Guillermo, please."

Guillermo was a rebel in the army and had displeased his superior who sent him to a very rural post where his major job was supervising the building of latrines. He was going crazy there. One day he picked up a medical magazine which advertised an essay competition in pediatric pathology. The winner would be awarded a year of training at the famous Children's Hospital in Boston. Desperate to get out of his exile, he entered and won the competition. He was full of mischief, and his prime target was Jose from Peru, a very short fellow who wore elevated shoes.

Although Guillermo appeared lackadaisical, he was a very dedicated pathologist, studying hard in his own area of interest, which was neuropathology. I would watch him spend many hours trying to perfect a special stain on neurofibrils. He was also not a man to be demeaned.

One day I was helping him show a chest surgeon a heart congenitally deformed. As soon as he began to speak in his Mexican accent, the surgeon took the heart from his hand and began to point out to us in a condescending let-me-teach-you manner, "This is the right atrium, the right ventricle, the left atrium, the left ventricle."

Guillermo interrupted and asked, "Do you think I went to a correspondence school for my medical degree?"

With that question unanswered, we both left the room for the surgeon to lecture to himself. I silently gave him three cheers.

Dean was a Canadian who was a veterinarian before becoming a doctor for humans. Still devoted to animals, he would make rounds at the animal hospital (coincidentally on the same street) before coming in to start his day at the hospital. He was a surgeon-in-training and had been unsuccessful in obtaining a residency in chest surgery at Children's, so he planned to spend the year in pathology, intent on doing something special enough to impress the group in chest surgery to allow him to join them. His wife, also a physician, was pregnant with their first child and was in an internal medicine residency at another Harvard-affiliated hospital. They were a wonderful couple— smart, cosmopolitan, fun-loving, and considerate. They warmly welcomed me into their circle, which brought me many hours of pleasure.

At work, Dean and I plotted how best to spend our spare time during work hours. We joined the Charles River Yacht Club, where we learned how to sail, and we attended religiously the famed weekly CPC (clinico-pathological correlation) of unusual cases at the Massachusetts General Hospital every Wednesday at noon, from where we would go to lunch at Durgin Park. Whenever possible, we would go to the Harvard Medical School to attend lectures in pathology given by the staff pathologists, who uniformly happened to be world-renowned in their specialty. Sitting among the students, I observed them with interest. They scraped and shuffled their feet collectively when the lecturer was not up to snuff, but when they thought the lecturer delivered to their satisfaction, they rewarded the teacher with a standing ovation.

I was reminded of my own student days. I had some very good teachers and some very bad ones. I would go to each class and pick a chair close to the door, and then I would give the teachers fifteen minutes to engage my interest. If they didn't, I would quietly slip out to do my own studying. I also had my share of "crazy" teachers. One I remember well taught us infectious disease. In this class, you had to have a quarter of a pad page with your name and a number he assigned you ready at all times for quizzes, which when given would include all subjects from the start of the course. When the first bell rang, which signaled a five-minute interval to dismissal, he would pick students randomly, like those who wore spectacles, to remain. He would then give the quiz question like "Classify cockroaches backward" or stand in front of you, stamping his feet yelling, "Come on, come on, the first one out gets an extra ten percent, last one out gets ten percent off." If you had a bad day or unprepared and couldn't answer the question of the day, he will call your name the next day, wave your quiz paper, and yell "zero" in front of the entire class. Talk about stress.

By comparison, I thought American students were treated quite decently.

Between all our activities at the hospital and the birth of his son and its aftermath of sleepless nights, Dean managed to garner the service of the hospital's illustrator to help him record a special type of hernia he noted in many of the children he autopsied. The findings were published in a prestigious surgical journal with him as the sole author. With that accomplishment, he became a shoo-in for the prized residency that he coveted.

Kato, a Japanese, was my roommate for the year. I actually cringed when I was placed beside him. My dislike for the Japanese stemmed from my wartime experience. So intense was my hatred that I could not bring myself to buy anything Japanese until well into the 70s. It was irrational, but it was there. Kato kept to his side of the room, intuitively acknowledging my antagonism. He did not go out of his way to engage me in conversations, and I did very little to encourage him. But since we were in the same room and I was ranked senior of the two and got paired to work with him, we slowly started to talk. First, we talked about the work we were doing, but as we became more comfortable with each other, the chats evolved into different aspects of our lives.

I found out that during the war, all the children in Japan were removed from their parents and sent into mountain retreats in case Japan was attacked. As he recounted his life during that period to me, I found myself for the first time sympathetic toward someone Japanese.

I did not share with him my miserable existence under the Japanese occupation. Reaching back in my memory to that period, I recalled that I was approximately seven years old when my mother took all three of us, an older sister and a younger brother and me, from Rangoon, Burma, where my father was stationed to Shanghai to visit my dying grandfather.

The Japanese already occupied Shanghai, but their presence did not affect us. We settled in the suburb of Shanghai near my aunt's house beside a dairy farm owned by a British couple. My grandfather, instead of dying, improved, which made my mother decide to stay a little longer. She enrolled my sister and me in an English school so we would not miss any schooling during our visit. As the end of that year approached and the next year started, two things happened that changed our lives. Pearl Harbor was attacked, and Japan invaded Burma. These two events trapped us in Shanghai, even though my grandfather died and we were free to leave.

We'd lost communication with my father, and the Japanese presence in Shanghai became a scourge of our existence. The Japanese harassed my mother constantly about why we were enrolled in an English school. This stopped only when she withdrew us from that school and enrolled us in a Chinese school where we had to raise the Japanese flag every morning and learn Japanese.

Every morning before we left for school, my mother would remind us not to write slogans on the wall, not to shout any slogans, and to be make sure we bow to any Japanese soldiers we met. She didn't need to remind us about bowing because we had witnessed a boy having his head split open by a soldier for not doing just that.

Our neighbors, the British couple who owned the dairy farm, was carted off to a concentration camp; and the property was occupied by the biggest Chinese collaborator in Shanghai. He surrounded himself with countless numbers of soldiers, almost all Chinese, guarding him. Fortunately for us, he had a young son our age who needed playmates and we were approached by the soldiers to fill that role. We enjoyed these visits mainly because of the many treats, not available to the general populace, that we were given.

While we were enjoying our special perks, the Japanese occupation force began to tighten their rule. Curfews were imposed during all times of the day and night and when that happened, people on the streets were trapped between cordoned off areas with no idea when they would be able to move again. Here we were very lucky. When we were caught in one of the curfews, the soldiers, whom we got to know pretty well by now, would be informed by my mother and would come looking for us to take us home.

Food shortages, particularly rice, became drastic because all available rice was confiscated for the Japanese troops. To compensate for this shortage, rations of cornmeal were handed out—one-half pound per person per day. To increase the weight of the cornmeal, sand was added to the mix. I was elected by the family to stand in line to get this ration because I was small for my age and cute. As everyone guessed, I was always pushed to the front of the line by sympathetic and generous people who felt sorry for me. My older sister would wait for me on the sideline to help me carry the load. While we were always the first to get our ration, a steady diet of cornmeal with sand resulted in a rapid deterioration of my health. I became so sickly that a family friend, a pediatrician, after examining me one day, said to my mother, "She is going to die if you don't leave Shanghai. She may die on the way, but at least, she will have a chance to survive."

I was old enough to understand what he was saying. He was trying to save my life. *If I live*, I thought, *I should do something like what he is doing. Saving lives.* Thus, the seeds of a future vocation were sown and, like fermenting yeasts, bubbled slowly along a path to fruition.

My mother's decision to escape Shanghai to unoccupied territory after that conversation was bolstered by a message delivered to her through underground channels by my uncle (my father's brother) who was officially an employee of the department of transportation but was in fact a secret agent in the Chiang's government. The latter was pushed by the Japanese invasion to relocate inland with Chungking as its capital.

The message was that my father had escaped Burma and had arrived safely to Chungking. My mother prepared our departure by telling friends and neighbors that we were leaving Shanghai to go to my grandmother's village down south. She sold everything she could in exchange for nine gold chains, the currency of choice during troubled times and war.

We would travel with an aunt and her four-year-old boy up to a certain point beyond the occupied territories, where we would part company. The plan was to take trains going south along the Japanese occupied east coast, and when asked by officials, we would always give the next stop as our destination.

On that long-awaited day, our friends, the soldiers again came to our rescue, escorting us to the train station, just in case a curfew was ordered. On arrival to the station, we discovered that our departure was delayed because the train we were taking was commandeered for some other use. This left us sitting at the station without any idea when we would be starting on our journey.

In the late afternoon, we finally got moving and arrived at our destination in a pitch-dark station lit by a couple of candles stuck to small tables on which our luggage was examined.

To avoid being lost in the dark, we held each other's hands in a chain-like fashion with the adults at each end and called each other's name in sequence up and down the chain, inching ourselves forward towards the lit areas.

We stayed overnight in the station like everyone else and took the next train.

Our travel by train was not easy. The trains had no schedule. They appeared when they appeared. It took us weeks to go nine hundred miles. My mother, while chatting with a fellow passenger, confirmed a fact not widely known. Along the east coast were small areas devoid of occupation forces— areas where escape would be possible. Ideally, that's where we needed to go. How to get to that exact area would require a great deal of luck. And luck was with us.

One day, our train broke down close to a station and all passengers were told to get out with their belongings and wait. Our little band of six drifted toward a wooden platform. Soon, vendors of all kinds, including a middle- aged man who lingered to chat, bombarded us. He told us he lived nearby and knew the area very well. This information brought an alert look on both the adults' faces. He went on in a nonchalant way to say that if someone wanted to escape to unoccupied territory, this was the exact spot to do it. My mother was afraid to trust him but managed a weak, "Is that so?"

The man offered to bring us to a boarding house, assuring us that we could always take another train. The adults consulted each other and decided to do as he suggested. When we got to our destination, the lady who greeted us at the boarding house gave us a big room. The kids would sleep together on the floor, and the adults would have the beds. My mother and auntie talked late into the night, debating whether the man could be trusted. They went back and forth discussing the possibilities of what could happen to us if he reported us to the Japanese. Neither of them slept well that night.

In the morning, the same lady beckoned us toward the kitchen and gave each one of us a bowl of soymilk for breakfast. My mother gingerly asked if she knew the man who brought us there. She said, "Yes, I have known him for twenty years. He is a good man. If you need help, let him help you. He will not harm you. He will be here in the early afternoon."

Buoyed by this, we all waited eagerly for the man's appearance.

When he finally arrived, he stepped into the house, not like that of a stranger but in a very familiar manner. We learned later that he was a relative of the boarding house lady and that he was once the "mayor" of the town but was now unemployed, trying to be useful to people like us.

He told us that he had picked us out of the crowd because we did not look like the usual peasants making trips between villages. He suspected from the beginning that we were looking for a way to escape. To allay our fears, he also told us that he had aided many others in their endeavor to escape, without any mishaps.

The plan he laid out was for us to leave the boarding house when it gets dark to a shed close to the train. He told us that the trains stopping there were supply trains that had to be unloaded by the soldiers stationed there, leaving the area devoid of sentinels during the unloading. That's when we should leave the shed and crawl across the rails and head toward the field covered by very tall grass that would hide us from being detected. Once we reached the grassy area, we should run as fast as we could for as long as we could in a straight line. We should keep moving until we were out of the grassy field into the free territory. What he didn't need to tell us was that if we were detected, we would likely be shot. He took us to the shed and bade us good- bye, wishing us luck.

While we waited for the train, we decided that auntie and her son would go first followed by my mother and sister, who will also pull the luggage, and then me and my brother. We should lie in wait for each other after we crawled over the rail. Then we would dash into the grassy field altogether. A sliver of moonlight allowed us to make out each other's forms.

My little cousin looked terrified. We tried to pretend to him it was a game and told him he had to be very, very quiet. He was the most obedient child I have ever met, and I have often wondered how his little four-year-old brain enabled him to adjust to all the tension.

Miraculously we were able to carry out what we planned without a hitch, and as we dashed into the tall grass and continued running, my sister and I took turns in carrying the four-year-old, piggyback.

When we were deep into the field, we decided to rest a bit. Unsure still about our chances of being caught, we forced ourselves to move on and on and on at a slower and slower pace until it was dawn and we saw the edge of the grass. Freedom at last, and despite our utter exhaustion, all four kids ran toward the clearing on top of a slope, which lead to a road below. On the slope sat a young boy eating a bowl of rice. We gathered around him mesmerized. We had not seen rice for a long, long time.

Our plan now was to head for Chungking on any form of transportation we could get. We rode on wheelbarrows and sailed in sampans (boats), which we had to help pull in low tide. When we couldn't find any form of transportation, we walked. Soon, auntie and her son left us for another destination.

Soon too we decided to remain in a hotel until we could contact father at the Ministry of Foreign Affairs in Chungking. My mother had two gold chains left, not enough for the entire trip but enough to get us to Hubei. When my mother finally made contact, my father promised to send money to the post offices for us to pick up at each of our stops to get us to Chungking. When my father escaped Burma, he was asked by a friend to bring a bottle of quinine for his family. When my father reached Chungking, he possessed only the clothes on his back and that bottle of quinine. We had lost everything we owned in Burma, and the government was too poor to compensate us for the loss. In fact, the government was too poor to pay officials adequately and the money sent to us to get us to Chungking came from the sale of the quinine capsules, one by one.

My health along the way improved dramatically. My weight increased, and I started exhibiting boundless amounts of energy. Our family friend, the pediatrician who predicted that I might survive the trip, would have been very pleased to see me so transformed.

Along our long travel, one incident remained with me clearly. We were staying in a hotel at the foot of a mountain. Very early every morning we would hear shouts followed by clapping. This piqued my curiosity, so together with several other kids we decided to explore this commotion. We got up early and left the hotel, joining a crowd of people forming a ring. In the middle of the ring was a blindfolded man kneeling. To our horror, we realized we were witnessing an execution. The shouting and clapping were aids for the dispersion of the soul of the executed. The scene was so gruesome that we ran as fast as we could back to the hotel, scared out of our wits. I never did dare tell anyone what I saw.

Finally, we were now on our last stop before reaching Chungking. Here, we had to wait for a bus to take us on a drive up a mountain with sixty-three sharp curves. Buses then, fueled by coal, were terribly unreliable and, again, had no particular schedule.

Unexpectedly before we could take that bus, we were tracked down by a man who handed my mother a letter written by my uncle, the one who was a secret agent but officially an employee of the department of transportation. He wrote that the man delivering the letter was a driver who was driving his truck back to Chungking after delivering a supply of pipes. We should ride with him because that would make our trip safer and much faster.

With great anticipation for the last leg of our journey after traveling through ten provinces, we boarded the truck. We arrived in Chungking in two days instead of the usual four to six. When we arrived, we went directly to the only hostel there and was told that no room was available. My mother pleaded with the manager, telling him that she had travelled three months with three children to get there. Moved by her obvious distress, he told us that he had a room where the renter never stayed for the night, although he would come in during the day. So, if we cleared the room during the day, we could then stay the night. My mother agreed immediately.

She then got on the phone to the Ministry of Foreign Affairs, trying to reach father. She was told that he hadn't been in for days, trying to pick his wife and children up on their arrival. While she was on the phone, my sister, standing outside of the hostel came in and said, "There is someone out there that looks like father." My mother dashed out and confirmed it was indeed him. The most amazing thing we learned was that the room given to us by the manager was actually my father's room. He had reserved it for our arrival.

The reunion with father did not last long. We found out that he lived in the foreign ministry's dorm and that his pay was inadequate to get us an apartment. While my parents grappled with this situation, my mother, with the slimmest of chance, bumped into a former colleague from Nanking University, a place where she once taught music. This man had become the head of an experimental school in Chengdu and was in Chungking looking for someone to head his department of music. He was overjoyed to see my mother and immediately offered her the job. With it came a free cottage and a salary of eight fifty-pound bags of rice per month. Due to inflation, money was not offered. Rice, a needy commodity, could be sold easily.

Once again, mother and three kids travelled to Chengdu to a school we all thought was paradise. It was located in a rural area with lots of trees and a river abutting it. Between the main school building and the teacher's cottages lay an expanse of land that took almost five minutes to traverse. The school had about two hundred handpicked, tuition-free students as guinea pigs on which various modes of teaching with untested curriculum were carried out. The aim of the school was to produce a uniformed, acceptable method of teaching with a standard curriculum for the whole province from grades one to six. Teachers were extremely innovative; students were too.

I like to tell the story about our first dinner at the school. Each table had ten students picked according to age. When the food was served, a bucket of rice was placed besides each table. A line would be formed to transfer rice from the bucket to the bowl in each student's hand. After we did this and returned to the table, I noticed that all the students except me had their bowls half full. I realized the significance of this when they all wolfed down their rice and went back to the bucket for the second time, with me still plowing through my share without any hope of getting a little more rice.

We were in that school for almost a year. My existence there was exhilarating. Every day was an adventure in learning, the likes of which I would never experience again, occurring in an environment that had no classroom desks, no standard blackboards, nor textbooks.

My father was transferred to Calcutta, India, in 1943. We left for India in a military transport flying over the Himalayas (the hump). The experience was so traumatic due to the air pockets that for weeks after we landed, I would become nauseous at the sound of a plane flying overhead.

Now back to Boston. I didn't think my Japanese office mate would have enjoyed hearing my story. At any rate, over time we became friendlier and he soon joined my circle of friends which included Dean and his wife. Together we found that being a doctor in Japan was pretty grim, earning less than taxi drivers at times. He confided that he would love to work in an American agency like the Atomic Energy Commission in Japan. Dean quickly reminded him that the most influential pathologist with the AEC worked in the hospital right across from us. He nagged Kato until Kato went to see this famous pathologist, who did obtain for him a position in Japan. We all felt pretty good about the outcome.

In the meantime, Dr. Volker decided to give a party for all of us at his home. I could not go because I was on call that evening.

Dean told me the next day that the party was god-awful. No one would say anything, not Dr. Volker nor his German wife nor any of those invited. Only Dean tried mighty hard to fill in these long periods of silence. It was so ghastly an evening for everyone that he wanted me to remind him never to do this again.

During this period too, strange things were happening within the department. Mary, our prim and proper unmarried secretary, was finding smutty letters addressed to her on her desk each morning. Words in the letter were made up of snippets from magazines or newspapers.

Also, slides selected for daily conferences were found with their coverslips removed and most disturbing, brain slices placed in fixatives for further examination were slashed into. Instantly, we all became detectives. We all agreed that this was an inside job. We also agreed that this was a very angry person. We eliminated Mary, the secretary, and the mother-and- daughter team in histology. Wade, the diener, was the only one left. He was an interesting person. Despite our rocky start, we got along well. He was a man who wanted us to see him as someone better than a diener, and he probably was. He would arrive at work on weekends with the *London Times* tucked under his arm. He knew a lot of pathology due to his long tenure in the department, and he often would upstage the junior residents by pointing out their errors. I was often surprised by his erudite explanation of some complicated financial matters exposed by the media. I learned that Wade had high hopes of being rescued from his job and promoted to something better by Dr. Farmer.

This hope was based on the fact that Dr. Farmer did just that for the diener before Wade. That person became the hospital's official scientific photographer by the good grace of Dr. Farmer even though he was generally a gofer still for our leader. It was also rumored that Dr. Farmer gave this favored man his used car every year. Wade had been in the department now for many, many years, and there had been no sign of any rescue.

A Tale Out of Season

Although Dr. Volker did mention that an investigation was being carried out to explain all the mishaps in the department, we saw no evidence of any action. Soon Christmas was on us, and parts of the department were decorated. The histology department had a very small synthetic Christmas tree around which a cutout "Merry Christmas" hung. One morning, the mother-and-daughter team found the words cut up with "Me Christ" remaining around the tree.

This particular occurrence unnerved many of us, who now had boyfriends and significant others sit with us when on call between 6:00 to 8:00 p.m. when the department was completely deserted.

Later, at a regional pathology meeting, I ran into a pathologist who had been at Children's the previous years. She asked me how things were going, and I recounted these strange occurrences to her. She nodded, totally unsurprised, and said, "I bought a beautiful plant for the conference room and someone killed it by watering it with formalin. I also had my bra cut up when I changed into scrubs to do a post in the evening. I always thought it had something to do with me being Jewish." She was a Hungarian immigrant, who still had a tattooed number on her forearm from her concentration camp days.

I was unhappy to hear this because, to me, this meant that what was happening was not new. We continued to ask Dr. Volker about the investigation, but his usual reply was, "Nothing new."

I believed that Wade was the prime suspect, but he was never uncovered, not in our year anyway. Another new year was upon us, and plans for the coming year needed attention again.

My parents at this time had moved from the Philippines to Hong Kong and joining them was a distinct possibility and so practicing there needed serious consideration. This included obtaining credentials recognized by Hong Kong. Instead of certification by the American Board of Pathology, I would need to be certified by the Royal College. The idea of going to Canada for a year and then take the exam seeped into my mind. On an impulse, I applied to the Children's Hospital in Montreal for another year of pediatric pathology, and my application was quickly accepted, and I was appointed a resident.

With this impulsive act, I had complicated my life a little bit more because several months down the road, I decided to get married. I had met this very handsome man who was asked by a mutual friend to bring me a package. He was a postgraduate student at Boston University. It was not love at first sight, but the attraction was there. Soon his mother flew from Taiwan to Hong Kong to meet my father, and soon they got involved to prod our friendship along a desired course. I learned (from my father) that he came from a very wealthy and very well-known family whose ancestry could be traced centuries back.

His father never worked a day in his life. He was a collector of sorts in paintings and special porcelain cups. The story is often told about how he would buy the entire production of a batch of these porcelain cups and break all of them except one. He also devoted himself to cultivating four acres of chrysanthemums solely for presentation at shows and owned a stable of horses for racing.

His mother's family was not shabby either. For her wedding, her father bought a chunk of jade from which her wedding jewelry and decorations for her wedding gown were carved. Her dowry stretched a mile. When she was bored and told her father that she wanted to work, he bought a third of a bank on the condition that she be put in a management position. This allowed her to direct an all-female bank at age twenty-two. In later years, she became a well-known arbiter in labor disputes in Shanghai.

Ten children, five girls and five boys, resulted from the marriage. My husband-to-be was number five. He was the most adventurous among his siblings. In a spate of discontent with family laced with patriotic fervor, he joined the Youth Army organized by the government to attract young men to service when he was sixteen. This Youth Army morphed into the New Sixth Army in which he took part in combat duties against the Japanese in Burma. His unit eventually came under the command of US General Joseph "Vinegar Joe" Stillwell. When the war ended, he was welcomed home as a hero with pockets stuffed with back pay that he recklessly gambled away at the first casino his eyes set on.

When the Communist took over mainland China, his father preferred to remain with his concubine while his family relocated to Taiwan. Not unexpectedly, he was incarcerated by the Communist for belonging to a class demonized for the ills of the country. He died of cancer while in prison. Despite the tradition of sons burying parents, all of the sons declined. A filial daughter made the hazardous trip back to China to bury him amid harassments, frightening intimidations, and temporary detention by the Red Guards.

Our relationship continued pleasantly and progressed as parents from both sides had hoped. We were married in the chapel within the Holy Trinity Lutheran Church in New York City attended by relatives and close friends.

Now I was faced with the choice of reneging on my Canadian contract or risk a losing fight with the US Immigration Department to remain in the country. I consulted many of my friends, including Dean, who were knowledgeable about Canadian affairs, to advice me on what I should do. I was warned not to renege on my contract because Canadians were very strict about honoring contracts, especially when I had to view this decision from the standpoint that I might be forced to go there at some later date due to my uncertain circumstances.

My husband and I decided to have a conversation with the immigration officials to find out the difficulties involved in remaining in this country. We were very lucky to meet a very sympathetic immigration officer who explained to us that a provision in my exchange student's visa required me to leave the country for two years. The possibility of reentering the country as an immigrant would depend on the quota for Chinese. Fortunately for me, he was willing to put me in the quota for Indonesians because I was born there, which favored a faster entry due to the fact that the Indonesian government at that time prohibited immigration to the US, leaving their quota unfilled.

With that information, the decision to go to Canada was made.

Once that decision was made and the possibility of returning to the US became a reality, I needed to prepare myself as a candidate to be eligible for the examination given by the American Board of Pathology. To be able to do that I needed to take a state medical licensure examination so that the board certification would be valid for recognition in the US. It was strongly rumored that foreigners who took the pathology board exam not based on any US medical license and taken only for the prestige of having the certificate to show off when returning home to practice would not have their certificate recognized if they returned to the US.

There were only a few states that permitted nonimmigrants to take these licensure exams. One of the states was Maine, which was close enough for me to get to. I applied for the licensure exam and plunged into reviewing the twelve subjects that would be tested over a period of two days, scheduled at Colby College in Waterville, Maine. The day of the test was a wintry day typical of New England. The snow was so deep on both sides of the road that driving along a pathway to the college gave me a tunneling effect.

The large examination room was filled with mostly foreign candidates. I had a Turkish man beside me who told me that he was taking this exam for the fourth time, rattling my self-confidence.

Before the examination, a representative from the Maine Board of Medicine appeared before us and made this encouraging statement, further increasing everyone's stress factor.

"Many of you have taken this test before, and many more will take it again. Good luck."

The test was difficult but reasonable. Unlike some other states, I thought it was not designed for failure so that the state could selectively pass only those whom it wanted to pass.

I passed. I could now practice medicine in the state of Maine, and I could now take the examination given by the American Board of Pathology on par with any American graduate. It was a giant step forward.

Back at Children's, Dean, being the friendly soul that he was, had friends among the Harvard medical students. They invited him to one of their dorm parties where the beer served was unusual in its taste and strength. He asked where the beers were purchased and was told that they had brewed it themselves in the dorm. Dean immediately pulled out a notebook and got the recipe. He met me the next day, very excited at the prospect of making our own beer. He told me that he had scouted around the lab and found the perfect receptacle for it. This turned out to be a large glass container with a narrow neck topped by a rubber stopper that had a hole in it, which was perfect for inserting a tube to let out unwanted air. I soon got caught up with the excitement and planned with Dean, Kato, and Guillermo on washing the container, purchasing the ingredients, and hiding the container from view.

Once that was done, we met one evening to concoct this brew. Dean was the obvious brewer in chief, measuring out the ingredients according to his recipe, while we helped him mix and pour the contents into the glass container. All this was being done in my room with Kato because the room conveniently had a door, which, when opened, would hide the container behind it preventing prying eyes from discovering our clandestine booty.

During the brewing process, we went around badgering each resident to bring in as many one-liter empty bottles as possible, explaining to them their purpose and requesting them to keep the bottles in their lockers.

Every morning, Dean and I would make "bubble" rounds, monitoring the progress of fermentation. When in doubt, we called in our consultants—the medical students.

In approximately a month, the fermentation was declared complete and the original four conspirators gathered on a weekend to bottle the beer with a borrowed bottle capper, naturally from the medical students.

The empty bottles were lined up in a row on a bench as we siphoned the beer into each bottle, remembering to add a pinch of sugar at the end before the capping. What we failed to remember was to draw the venetian blind over the windows that faced the office of the chief pathologist of the Peter Bent Brigham Hospital.

Between capping the bottles, I happened to raise my head and, to my horror, saw the chief pathologist across the street watching us, shaking his head and wagging his finger at me. I detected a smile on his face before I quickly lowered the blinds without making any remarks about what I just witnessed. I asked the men to hurry up in case we got raided.

We brought all the bottles back to the lockers, allowing the sugar to continue the fermentation process for another week before sharing it with everyone. Dr. Volker received a complimentary bottle decorated by a ribbon. He did not look surprised, neither did he ask us where we got the beer. He gave us the impression that he knew all along what we had been up to. He did, however, compliment us on the taste and the strength of our concoction, claiming that he was knocked out cold after a glass.

Dean also found out two bits of news about Dr. Volker. He was having a birthday in a week, and at the same time, he was being considered for a promotion to associate professor of pathology at the Harvard Medical School, a very big deal. Dean gathered us together and suggested that we give him a party and present him with a "Harvard" chair to express our hopes that he will one day "chair" the department. We all agreed and dutifully handed over money that we couldn't afford for the present. The party was held in the lab, modest in nature but big in success. Dr. Volker was visibly touched.

The year was definitely coming to an end. In appreciation, Dr. Volker decided to invite us again to his house for dinner. He tacked the invitation onto the bulletin board with a blank piece of paper attached to it for us to sign up. One week passed and the blank sheet remained blank, embarrassing us, but no one wanted to go.

Dr. Volker got the message. The following week he switched his invitation from home to Pier Four, a famous restaurant along the waterfront, and within an hour, the blank page was filled with everyone's name.

We had a wonderful time at Pier Four, and Dr. Volker was forced to part company with a large wad of cash.

We said our farewells at the end of the year, and although we promised to keep in touch, Dean and Kato were the only two I had a chance to meet briefly in the course of our professional lives.

I was now headed for Canada.

Canada in general is quite similar to the US, except for the part that is French, which is where I landed. This area of the country definitely exuded a distinct and special flavor. The 1960s was not a particular good time for French Canadians. Their desire to have a special status within Canada had not been met with success from the rest of the country and talks of separation from Canada raged on, culminated by General de Gaulle's famous controversial cry in Montreal, "Viva le Quebec libre" (Long live free Quebec). Tension between French and English Canadians could be found in their daily exchanges, exposed as petty expressions of their dislike for each other.

I, however, found the Canadians generous in their treatment of their resident staff, in a much more humane way than their US counterpart. The living quarters were more than adequate in size; the food was excellent; there was a big common room in the dorm, where a piano sat with card tables, a TV, and comfortable sofas.

Best of all, we received four weeks off for vacation time instead of the standard two weeks in the US.

The department consisted of two staff pathologists: the chief, who was a small dapper man with a mustache and an ever-present carnation in his lapel, and his associate chief, Humphrey, a huge burly Englishman.

There were four residents: me, a married Brazilian woman who lived at home, and two male pediatric residents rotating through pathology.

I was back doing autopsies, except in this institution, I had to stop and ask for the chief to come in and look at every abnormality I found. Since I felt I was experienced enough to know what I was doing, I did not accept this unnecessary, exasperating standstills willingly. I made this clear by my facial and body movements that I abhorred this nonsense. The chief soon came to the conclusion that I was competent enough and exempted me from this unreasonable practice.

The chief and Humphrey, his associate, shared microscopic reading of the surgicals. I was privy to the surgicals only through Humphrey, who always displayed his gruff side to hide his extreme likability. He drove a VW Beetle, and many a days, I would find him bent over, working on his VW, with parts scattered all over his desk.

He was great fun to talk with, and I liked him a lot. The chief, like all his counterparts in other hospitals, soon decided to give us a welcome party. I do not recall his house, but I do remember what he served. It was a large baked whole salmon (head included) that was the most delicious that I have ever tasted. We ate in a room that included his beautiful orchids, cultivated in incubators reserved for human babies. The incubators were lit, and when the lights went off at a specific time during the evening, the chief turned his head toward his orchids and said "good night". I tried my hardest to muffle a laughter gurgling in my throat when I caught sight of Humphrey trying to do the same.

Later, as Humphrey drove a few of us home, he regaled us with stories of the chief dancing on a piano top at a faculty party when he had had one too many a drink. He was definitely not the austere, proper man he seemed to be. After a few months, the chief decided he could trust me after all, and this trust extended to asking me to project slides for him during his lectures. I was happy to oblige, and the first time I did it, I brought along a novel to read in between projecting his slides. This apparently insulted him enough for him to complain to Humphrey, who told me to "Carry on."

As my relationship with the chief smoothed itself out with civility, he encouraged me to present a paper at a regional pathology meeting to be held in a month's time. With his help in picking a topic, I managed to put together a paper titled "Plasma Vasculosis" and presented it to the members. It was warmly received, although I had great doubts that it contributed to their understanding of this little-known entity. The chief remarked later that he was amazed that I did not exhibit any nervousness during my presentation. I told him that I was able to do that only because I had convinced myself that the audience was all French and could not understand a word I said. Humphrey was greatly amused by my confession and ribbed me about it all day.

Between my established work schedule, I looked forward to going to NY on the weekends at least once a month to join my husband who was working then in New York.

It was during one of these trips that the landlord of the building came pounding on our door about President Kennedy's assassination. We immediately became transfixed to our radio, getting all the terrible news.

That evening, we decided to go out for a walk. The streets everywhere had this eerie silence where groups of people gathered to whisper their thoughts. It reminded me of a wartime pattern of human behavior where strangers gathered to console each other, all wearing a universal cloak of sadness.

I watched the burial ceremonies back in Canada with all the other residents glued to the TV sets during every spare moment we had.

It was a time of shared pain and regrets, bearing witness to John John's unforgettable salute and Robert Kennedy's unbearable grief.

My life fell into a rhythm of sorts. After work each day, I would drift down to the common room, a central area for after-work activities. Bridge players who were all on call always occupied the card table.

As soon as one was called, another from the room would step in. I occasionally found myself at the table when no one else could fill in.

There were always people sitting on sofas studying, seriously studying, for examinations taking place two to three years hence. The most studious one present was a gentleman pointed out to me as someone who was a gold medal graduate from the University of Hong Kong. He had already completed his study of six textbooks and was in the process of doing it again for the second time. I, by comparison, had about four textbooks I had to go through, and I had barely started.

Impressed by their diligence and by my own awareness that I should be preparing for my examination seriously too, I joined this group, concentrating on studying for at least three hours each night.

One evening, I noticed a number of strangers popping in and out of the room and going toward a boxlike Coca Cola machine near the door. I learned that this machine was stocked with beer, operated by the resident staff for petty cash to meet our needs. This bit of entrepreneurship brought us a great deal of money because it was the sole supply of beer to the neighborhood in the evening. This also explained the large amount of amenities offered to us in the common room.

When weekends came, I either stayed or took a train to New York.

Friendship within the department was limited, but dorm mates offered a larger circle of opportunity. We were a mix of men and women from all parts of Canada and US. Most of them were pediatrics residents. One such resident, a woman, became a good friend. She was named Doris, and she was unique in the sense that she volunteered to go every other month to Eskimo country, under Canada, to serve as its health expert. While there, she would pull out teeth, deliver babies, do minor surgery, and treat all kinds of disorders. One of her patients was a famous soapstone bird sculptor who was afflicted with a large skin cancer. He visited her periodically to get pain medications, and with each visit, he would present her with one of his sculptured birds. They were beautiful and sold for very high prices everywhere in Canada.

On one of her returns to our residence, Doris somehow found out my birth date and invited me to dinner that day. She would not divulge where she was taking me, but she did ask me not to order the steak.

We got on a bus and got off close to the Queen Elizabeth Hotel, one of the most expensive places in town. To my surprise, she led me into the hotel and into the dining room, where we were ushered to a table for two. I looked around and saw that we were definitely the youngest diners. We were also not dressed well enough because every woman in the room had an animal around her neck.

When I read the menu, I realized why I was asked not to order the steak. The price of that item was astronomical. The cheapest dish offered was chicken, which I decided to have. Doris also chose something similar.

Before ordering our meal, we were approached by the wine captain. When we politely refused any wine, he bent down close to us and said in a very soft and kind voice, "You can order a half bottle, you know." We were both sorry we had to disappoint him.

It was a very elegant and memorable dinner. After which, Doris also gave me a beautiful soapstone bird carved by her special patient, a gift that I treasure to this day.

Christmas was approaching, and Christmas always seemed to energize people. This was especially true at the hospital where a tradition demanded Christmas entertainment to be provided by the resident staff in exchange for a lavish buffet dinner hosted by the medical staff.

Planning for this event started with a meeting of the resident staff, and newcomers like me learned how this was going to be done. A committee would plan and write the play, and another would pick the players. Related small groups in the play would meet to practice whenever they could, and the first time that everyone would be together to enact the entire play would be on the day before it would be shown to the medical staff. That would act like a rehearsal, and the nursing staff would be our guests.

We had four weeks to do this. I was not picked for anything, and I never saw anyone rehearsing. I had no idea how this play was progressing, but soon the big day was upon us. Our common room was transformed into a theater. All members of the medical staff had preferred front row seats while we filled the back. The air was filled with excitement and anticipation.

The curtain opened, and the stage was seen decorated as in a cabaret. A lone musician in a corner rendered a soulful "La Vien Rose" on his trumpet, luring a pair of dancers to slither onto the stage, moving and swaying into an upright position in perfect synchrony with the music, a picture so sexy and seductive that the audience stood and cheered. This act was followed by a line of men entering dressed in hula skirts below and decorated with coconut shell breasts above. They performed a fantastic hula dance with the grace and lithe comparable to the best hula dancers anywhere. We were further treated to skits skewing the trials and tribulation of hospital life and a thorough roasting of the stuffiest members of the staff with wit and sarcasm. The night was a tour de force, brandishing the incredible talents of all who took part in this presentation, talents secretly buried beneath white coats and serious demeanors. Following the entertainment came the unbelievable lavish buffet served in the same room on a giant horseshoe-shaped table decked with a variety of sumptuous foods including oysters from Nova Scotia, served by tuxedo-clad experts, prying open each shell with aplomb. Drinks flowed *ad libitum*. The medical staff had by this time disappeared to the various parts of the hospital, coverings for all the residents on call for that night.

I had never seen anything like it, and I was again impressed by the Canadian's unusual fraternal attitude toward their resident staff.

It was that time of the year again to assess my path forward. I had had five years of training in anatomic pathology, suitable for a job within academic settings. To work in a community hospital, however, an expertise in clinical pathology would be required. With that in mind, I secured another year of residency at the same institution in clinical pathology.

The next few months were not remarkable until a ten-year-old girl was admitted unconscious to the hospital. The family lived in a shed in the woods, and the parents could not give any information helpful toward a definitive diagnosis. Clinically she appeared to be having some kind of encephalopathy (brain disorder) but the cause was unknown. She was placed in the intensive care unit, hooked up to life-preserving devises, and treated by broad- spectrum antibiotics.

The child continued to deteriorate. The intern in charge of the case reinterviewed the parents over and over trying to pry some bits of useful information but all for naught until he asked them if they owned any animals. They didn't, but the father suddenly recalled that the girl had awaken one night several weeks ago and complained that she had been bitten by a small animal, a squirrel maybe. The intern immediately thought of the possibility of rabies and rushed back to ICU to check on his patient, but he was too late. The patient was in extreme respiratory distress and died soon after.

When she was brought to the autopsy suite, the possibility of rabies had not been entered into the chart. As far as I could gather from her clinical history, she had died of encephalopathy of unknown origin. I began the autopsy, and halfway through, the chief burst into the room in an agitated state and told me that the case may be rabies. He informed me that he would remove the brain and we would do an immediate frozen section on the brain matter to identify the Negri bodies, a diagnostic feature of rabies.

I finished the examination and saw the chief entering the room gowned and masked like a Martian to perform his task. Negri bodies were indeed identified by frozen section on a section of the brain. The child had died of rabies. The hospital's administrative staff went into overdrive. They identified sixteen people, including me, who had been exposed to the dead girl. Despite the fact that human-to-human transmission of rabies is extremely rare, the decree from above was that all those exposed would be vaccinated. We were lined up daily and vaccinated with the old vaccine of inactivated rabies virus grown in duck embryo. These injections were extremely painful and were delivered to the abdomen for up to twenty-three days.

I developed many of the side effects associated with this vaccine. Each time I had a new injection, all the previous sites of injections would flare up resulting in red blobs all over my belly. In addition, I had muscle aches and a low-grade fever that persisted throughout this ordeal. It was a miserable experience.

To add insult to injury, the hospital appealed to us to contribute our blood for the sake of science after each injection for the determination of antibodies. The chief was not in this group. He either refused to be included or was convinced that his protection was adequate.

In July, I started on my clinical pathology training assigned to microbiology first, rotating later to hematology, chemistry, and blood banking. In each of these areas, I basically worked like a technologist, performing the tests.

Microbiology, located at the top floor of the hospital, presented us a height suitable for spotting fires around the neighborhood and enabling us to report it to a radio station as a side benefit. This brought in small rewards that kept us enjoying this particular sport.

Hematology, chemistry, and blood banking rotations were tedious slogs.

The tedium was suspended when I found out a month later that I was pregnant, complicating my life further. It wasn't the best time for the joys of parenthood. While I agonized over the choices, I had to make regarding the birthplace of the baby for fear of complicating an immigration problem that was already complicated enough, I received a letter from Dr. Dunham, the pathologist at Lowell, who had befriended me. He was coming to Canada to see me. When he did, he took me to a very fancy French restaurant and surprised me by offering me a job as his assistant. He also offered to be the sponsor for my immigration process. This was like manna from heaven, so I gratefully accepted the offer immediately.

I knew Dr. Dunham badly needed help and that his reluctance in finding help stemmed from his past experience of being ousted from his former job. This latter fact was related to us by his wife Barbara who claimed that his former colleagues were a nasty bunch who could not compete with his superior intellect.

Being mostly a guest in his house and an intern at work, I probably gave him an impression that it was a good bet that I would be malleable to his suggestions and agreeable with him on most matters, thus, a good choice for him.

Bernardo, whom I last saw with his wife at my wedding, the only close friends I had invited, wrote me that he was now at Yale doing a fellowship in cardiovascular radiology. When he learned that I was pregnant and, in a dilemma, as to where I should have the baby, he suggested that I stay with them and have the baby in the US.

Another problem solved.

The last problem involved the timing of the birth to be within my four weeks off. This still required that I be positioned under my lucky star, and that I obtain some cooperation from the baby as when it chose to say hello to the world.

Many of my dorm mates watched my expanded girth with shared happiness. At a dinner one evening, one of the men looked at me slyly and said in a singsong voice, "I know what you have been doing." I answered without losing a beat, "I have the license for that, you know," which set him off roaring with laughter.

Everything seemed to be falling in place. I decided to take my four-week vacation starting April 17. Bernardo arranged an obstetrician for me, and the Dunhams volunteered to care for the baby while I finished my residency. My husband planned to move from New York to Massachusetts to stay close to the baby.

On that fateful day, Bernardo and his wife received me warmly into their home in Connecticut, and within five days I was at the Grace New Haven- Yale Medical Center having the baby, a normal, healthy beautiful girl. Severe vomiting attributed to Demerol and a fairly severe case of postpartum depression complicated my postpartum period. I returned to Canada without the baby but was comforted by the fact that my husband had relocated to Massachusetts and actually found an apartment next to the Dunhams where he saw the baby every day.

On some weekends, I would visit husband and baby but the trip back to Canada was gut-wrenching and often resulted in a flood of tears.

I could not get back to the US fast enough.

I reentered the United States on a propitious day, September 23rd, the date of my husband's birthday. It was a time of great joy and celebration. We were together again, ready to begin our new journey in a new land of our choice. We both had new jobs, a new apartment, and a new baby. This new life was starting out in pretty good shape. Barbara, Dr. Dunham's wife, who had been taking care of the baby, insisted that she should keep the baby during the week for a while and that we could take over during the weekends. She also insisted that we not use the many beautifully embroidered underwear we received from parents and friends for the baby but instead use a specific American brand, Carter's, which we had to go to Needham to get. The thermal blankets we had received as gifts were not useful either. We needed to use woolen ones. Although these edicts appeared inflexible, we did not think it was unreasonable since we knew nothing about raising a baby and she was the expert.

One thing did bother me. We often visited the baby after work when she was put to bed. Often too, we would stay for a while and had to endure listening to the baby crying all the time we were there, up to an hour. Barbara assured us that crying was good for the lungs, but I thought it pretty cruel. Despite my strong feelings, I did not dispute her thesis. There was not much I could do to alter the situation anyway. I certainly could not replace her, she being the wife of my boss who just gave me a job and sponsored my entry to the United States.

I started work almost immediately. Driving to the hospital on a beautiful autumn day, the kind treasured by all New Englanders, warmed in the sun with a hint of winter in the shades, my heart took a leap of joy as the familiar outlines of the hospital came into view. This was homecoming, a full circle victory lap. While idling to a stop in the parking lot, I made a fervent wish that my first job would be a success.

The receptionist greeted me like a long-lost friend. Previous mentors, now colleagues, welcomed me similarly. Dr. Dunham made room for me by adding a chair to a desk in his room, but before I could settle into my new job, I had to leave to take my American Board of Pathology examination in St. Louis.

I didn't have much trouble with this, thanks to my studious Canadian friends who inspired my diligent preparation. Passing this examination made me a specialist, but it did not permit me to practice medicine in Massachusetts. For that, I needed to pass the state board exam.

Graduates of foreign medical schools then did not have the privilege of reciprocity (the right to practice medicine in multiple states after passing a single set of exams) enjoyed by graduates of US medical schools. We had to take the state medical examination for licensure in every state in which we wanted to practice medicine. Presently, foreign medical graduates can take an examination called FLEX to obtain limited reciprocity.

Since preparation for taking the state medical licensure examination required again studying twelve basic subjects for a three-day exam and since I was allowed to practice in a limited sense (i. e., sending out reports under Dr. Dunham's signature), I elected to postpone this task.

Although the medical staff welcomed me back, regretfully at times, they remembered me as the intern they once knew, forgetting that I had returned after six years of additional training in pathology. They treated me dismissively when it suited them as if I were still an intern, ignoring my diagnosis when they felt Dr. Dunham knew better.

I discovered, to my great surprise, that Dr. Dunham never went to any local or national pathology meetings and never read any pathology journals. He didn't believe they were useful. The only sources of reference for him were standard textbooks of pathology, which were usually two years behind in providing up-to-date information. He had this firm belief that he was a good pathologist and that was that. Besides, who was there to contradict this conviction? Added to all the adjustments I needed to make at work, I was forced to deal with a chief tech named Will who appeared from the first moment I showed up as the assistant pathologist to be competing with me to see who was more important to Dr. Dunham. He would repeatedly stress to me that he was by saying "Dr. Dunham and I decided to…" on major decisions in the lab. When Dr. Dunham went on his vacation, I found that Will did that too without letting me know.

If Dr. Dunham was aware of Will's odd behavior, he made no comment about it to me. Instead, he acted as if Will had the right of way.

His gifted son had graduated from Andover at the age of sixteen and entered Yale as a sophomore. In his junior year there, he decided, for whatever reason, to flunk out. Yale, in recognition of his talents, advised him to try to do something worthwhile for a year, after which, Yale might be persuaded to readmit him. The something worthwhile turned out to be a job in our lab doing technical work.

He was quite capable of doing the work and his father would often praise his efforts. But father and son were having troubles of their own because during his period in the lab, Robert went out of his way to form a bond with Will which became tighter and tighter. So much so that he moved out of his own home and in with Will's family.

With that in the background, I realized I had a snowball's chance in hell to think Dr. Dunham would even try to persuade Will to change his behavior. My personal relationship with Dr. Dunham coasted along a rocky path destined for termination.

A Tale Out of Season

Barbara was an excellent babysitter, and she was very unhappy about the way we were taking care of the baby during the evenings and on weekends. She complained that it took her until Wednesday each week to bring the baby back to her schedule, which was very strict. Every day, from 8:00-9:00 a.m., the baby was placed outside in the playpen. From 9:00-10:00 a.m., they had a walk with the dog, when the baby would give a dog biscuit to the dog and one to herself to eat, related to us by Barbara with a tolerant smile. From 10:00-11:00 a.m., it was time for gardening, where the baby learned before she was two, the names of all the plants, in Latin. Then there was lunch, a nap, and more timed activities until Dr. Dunham got home before me to have his afternoon cocktail and to relieve the missus to make dinner.

We could not keep Barbara's daily schedule intact, because weekends were for catching up, trying to do all the things we couldn't do during the week. We tried our hardest to keep some parts of her schedule like naptime and bedtime. When the baby refused to sleep, we would put her in our car and drive around and around until she slept. We would take her for a walk in the stroller whenever we could, but then I was accused by Barbara of not dressing her in warm enough clothes for the weather. Barbara had lots of complaints about me as a mother, and she carried her complaints to her husband, who in turn conveyed the complaints to me at work. I would get home and complain to my husband, who then went to her in the evening to apologize. This circular path of unhappiness expanded like a pebble dropped into water until one day I came home from work to pick up the baby and found her with swollen lips. Recognizing this as an allergic reaction, I acted a bit panicky, frantically searching for my car keys, and told Barbara I needed to take the baby at once to the pediatrician.

I dashed out, raced to the pediatrician's office where the allergic reaction was confirmed, and a dose of adrenaline was administered.

In reviewing what could have happened, I knew the baby had a habit of saying, "Taste?" whenever she saw anyone eating or drinking. I also knew that Dr. Dunham always had a gin and tonic when watching the baby while Barbara was cooking dinner, and I guessed what could have happened was that he gave her a taste of his drink. Juniper berries in gin are known to produce allergies.

Dr. E. Mei Shen

Since he never mentioned what I suspected occurred, this episode brought on a massive protest from Barbara, who insisted the next day that I inspect all her kitchen cabinets to prove that she possessed nothing that could have caused the allergy.

At work that day, Dr. Dunham chastised me for behaving in a manner suggesting an emergency, which distressed his wife. He furthered went on to suggest that I was being melodramatic in my action but stopped abruptly when I said, "She was given adrenaline."

I started to park myself in the library for long hours to avoid sitting in a room with him at work. We did not have separate offices.

I began to seriously assess my career. Was I moving forward in any way? Definitely not. I was not even standing still. I was going backward.

At the same time, I was constantly being criticized as a pretty incompetent mother. I came to the conclusion that I was not one of those women who "could have it all." I was at the moment full of resentment. I resented starting work each day with a litany of what I had done wrong with my own child directed at me by Barbara through her husband. I resented that my husband felt the need to apologize to Barbara for my "transgressions." I resented the fact that it was the director of the hospital and not my boss who said while in an elevator with me, "The staff says a lot of nice things about you, and I think it's time for you to get a raise." Most of all, I resented playing second fiddle to Will's (the chief tech) opinions. I was definitely not in a good place.

Being a woman and the only female on the staff did not help either. I had no one to go to who could understand my problems at work. Neither did I have any close friends nearby whom I could confide in. There appeared to be no good way I could deal with Barbara's consistent criticisms other than fire her. If we did that, where would we find another babysitter? Andover is an affluent town where wives and mothers all stayed at home with no need for babysitters. Would I still have a job if we dismissed Barbara?

One way out of all this angst would be for me to quit. Quit work altogether. But then what? Stay at home and be the "perfect" mother according to the gospel of child care set out by Barbara? Do I throw all the education and training that I've had just to satisfy Barbara's complaints? It would seem like cutting off my nose to spite my face.

A Tale Out of Season

My review of past events from the time I arrived in this country to the present did not relieve me of my indecision as to whether I should or should not quit working. I still could not rid myself of the words "What to do?" echoing in my consciousness.

I finally came to the conclusion that I did not have the right to make this decision alone, so I broached this delicate subject of quitting work altogether so I could take care of my child properly to my husband one evening. He thought I was crazy to think up something like that. It was totally illogical. All the years I put in training? If I couldn't work with Dr. Dunham, I should leave him and go somewhere else. As for taking proper care of the baby, we were doing just that, even if Barbra didn't think we were. His forceful arguments against my idea made sense, and although I still had a lot of doubts about the outcome of my decision not to quit, I finally agreed with him. I give him full credit for saving my career.

Free of this burden that I had felt so depressed about, accompanied by so many sleepless nights, I began to form a plan. I will visit my old mentor Dr. Mann and ask him for a teaching position. That way, I would have access to a second opinion when Dr. Dunham and I disagreed on a diagnosis and, thus, rescue part of my self-confidence. A teaching job would also take me partly away from an environment that was no longer pleasant. In addition, I planned to have a very frank talk with Dr. Dunham to try to straighten things out; after all, I was going to end my second year with him soon and I wanted to correct some basic misconceptions about me.

I obtained a teaching appointment from Dr. Mann, which would require me to spend two mornings a week at the medical school. I also managed to schedule a talk with Dr. Dunham, which lasted three hours in his home one evening. Barbara did not join us, sensing a need for us to be alone. Although this was a difficult task for me, I realized this would be the one chance I have to be brutally frank. So, I gave him detailed evidence of all that I thought was wrong, including overt ill will from staff physicians, especially from an influential internist, who was incensed that all his skin lesions were always diagnosed as a keratoses of one kind or another. I assured him that I was not out to undermine him and stressed that he really needed to devote some effort to providing better diagnostic service to satisfy the staff. He listened with little comment even though he made sniffing sounds to convey his distaste for my opinion. I ended my monologue hoping that my harsh words banished from him any notion that I was a malleable piece of putty, easily molded into whatever he wanted me to be.

Dr. Dunham did not give any serious consideration to my complaints. Nothing changed.

I had baby number two, another beautiful girl, after a twenty-month gap. I was not getting any younger, and two children, close in age, was in my view a good choice. Barbara initially agreed to take care of both but declined after she saw the amount of money we offered. For the first child, the weekly cost was half of my husband's weekly salary. The care was, without a doubt, excellent; but when the second child came along, we did not offer twice the amount. This ended our connection to Barbara. And with that, all social interactions ceased between the two families.

I had to take my vacation time to stay home while we searched for a new babysitter. This was the first time I had the baby all day, and although I enjoyed taking care of her, I also had to admit that the job was not as easy as it looks and that working full-time had its merits. The new babysitter we finally found was not as learned as Barbara, but she suited our needs. She was a widow with grown-up children who did not require her to be home at a certain time to fix dinner. She also did not drive, which meant she had to be picked up every morning and driven home every evening. My children, under her care, could tell you in detail everything that happened on all the soap operas on TV. She was generally reliable, but periodically, she would leave me in a lurch, deciding to spend some time with her daughter. And as usual, I would take my vacation time until she came back.

At the medical school, I was assigned a permanent group of students for two hours twice a week throughout the school year. The change in landscape, among the students in my absence, was astounding. Students who uniformly used to be clad in white coats with shirts and ties in class now appeared in all kinds of garb. One wore a mailman's uniform throughout the year. Another wore flip-flops.

They all had a disheveled look about them, but their minds were quite sharp, and their passion against the Vietnam War was intense. Many of them would spend all their free time joining groups in protest, so much so that the department of pathology for the first time did not give a final examination at the end of the year out of consideration for the protesters, who were all ready to forego the exam to continue their protests. For me, the student's protests were affirmation of my own abhorrence of the war.

The Vietnam War was tearing apart the fabric of American families, and my own US-born distant relatives were not exempt from this turmoil. These distant cousins, both brothers, were drafted for the war. The younger one managed to give his examiner the impression that he was mentally unstable and was therefore exempted. The older brother disapproved his brother's deceit and went bravely to the Vietnam War. He spent an entire year in a tank and was the only one in his company who returned home all in one piece. On return, he was unable and unwilling to communicate with anyone for a year and a half, continued to eat only cold food that he became accustomed to eating, and broke off his relationship with a lovely medical student. Still, he was one of the lucky ones. He recovered from his long depression and went on to live a productive normal life.

Teaching had become a haven for me, a protective shield from all the problems at work. My two hours with the students consisted of showing them microscopic sections of representative pathological disorders they had just been lectured on. At times I would bring in corresponding gross specimens to show them. At the end of the year, each student appeared for a fifteen-minute oral exam that included microscopic diagnosis.

The year ended on a high note for me when the students presented me with a bottle of wine in appreciation. Many a times during the year at the medical school, I would visit Zack, my mentor in surgical pathology at the medical center, to show him cases in dispute. Gradually, I regained my confidence.

Another benefit I experienced at the medical school was meeting other pathologists from community hospitals scattered all over the Commonwealth. We usually gathered either before or after the teaching period to chat and compare notes on various subjects. One day, one of them chatting with me, casually asked "Are you happy where you are? If not, come and see me."

Another gift from above, bestowed in such a timely fashion.

Thus, I began my new life in another hospital north of Boston, in a city which had General Electric as their biggest employer and the hospital as the next biggest.

This hospital had about three hundred or so beds and was a teaching hospital, very much like that of Mount Auburn Hospital. It had a medical staff close to two hundred physicians, including one woman, a pediatrician. I became the second woman on the staff. The paucity of women on medical staffs surprised me. When I delved into the history of women's entry into the medical profession in the US, I found it occurred around the mid-nineteenth century as medical colleges for women were established in Boston, New York, and Chicago. Even though women could be educated in medicine, they could not participate in any clinical training. No hospital would admit them to their staffs, and no medical societies would recognize them. So after more than a hundred years after Dr. Elizabeth Blackwell's efforts to advance women in the field of medicine, women made up only 5.5 percent of medical school enrollment in 1949. By contrast, I graduated in a class in which women made up 24 percent in 1958.

When I visited this "new" hospital for my initial interview, I found the department of pathology on the ground floor, which was physically divided into two halves. One side had offices with secretaries alongside them. This area was attached to a common sign-out room with adjoining resident's room, conference room, a histology section, and a surgical cutting room. The other half was occupied by clinical pathology commonly referred to as the lab, the largest section of which belonged to chemistry, followed in size by hematology and microbiology. The blood bank and the nuclear medicine formed a sideward extension. The autopsy suite was located in the basement, which also had additional office space.

The instruments I saw in every division of the lab were the most up-to-date models available. Most impressive of all were the newest chemistry instrument that turned out twelve tests in a minute and the camera that had just been installed in nuclear medicine, the first of its kind on the north shore. It surprised me to find nuclear medicine in the pathologist's domain, having been brainwashed that anything dealing with imaging belonged by birthright to the radiologists.

Joining the department, I was at the lowest rung of four.

The chief, Henry, was a well-known, experienced, and excellent pathologist who had been at the hospital for about twenty-five years. Lewis, fifteen years younger, was the associate chief. He was a very, very smart man who was shy and quiet and was mainly involved with the clinical lab where his special skills allowed him to rule with unrivaled authority. He was also in charge of nuclear medicine where he prepared the isotopes used for diagnostic purposes.

When I expressed to Lewis my surprise at finding this new imaging technology in the department of pathology, he explained that the lab was where isotopes were first used and so this part of nuclear medicine was just an extension of what we had been doing. The only difference is that we were producing an image instead of a number.

Nuclear medicine as a specialty was in its infancy, especially in the use of a camera to capture images of organs under study outlined by isotopes. Lewis wanted me to be involved in this area, thus, persuading me soon after I joined the department to take a four-week course in nuclear physics given by the Atomic Energy Commission in Oak Ridge, Tennessee. I would have to leave my husband with the children, but he was very supportive and urged me to go.

There I learned the Southern version of hospitality with their "Come back now, y'all" and a bit of Oak Ridge's history during the period when scientists in the Manhattan Project gathered there. Fearful that the neighboring farmers would detect their real purpose, the scientists adopted farm words they would use in public when discussing their work. Hence a *barn* was the diameter of an atom, and a *cow* was a mother source of an offspring isotope. Terms we still use today.

At Oak Ridge, we were taught about the isotopes used in clinical situations, their half-lives, their ability to target an organ when attached to specific agents such as iodine for the thyroid.

We solved physics problems with our slide rules, which would be considered quaint today. In the last week of our studies, we saw patients and viewed nuclear images of their livers, bones, brains, lungs, and thyroid.

I learned enough to have a good foundation, and I soon joined Lewis and Jack in running the department. Jack was a radiologist interested in nuclear medicine who asked his chief to convince Lewis to allow him to be part of the department.

Matt, our third pathologist, was a tall handsome bachelor who owned a Jaguar and drove designing women within a five-mile radius gaga. He was closest to my age and had joined the group right after his training.

In our group of four, Henry did a great deal of administrative work, attending meetings of various kinds with the medical staff, as well as with the hospital administrators, who determined our budget, equipment requirements, and lab staffing needs. Matt and I did most of the daily work of surgicals and posts with little participation or responsibilities in running the lab, even though Matt was fully qualified, certified in both anatomic and clinical pathology.

For the first time I was sending out reports under my own name having acquired the necessary Massachusetts license to practice medicine. Signing out surgicals was again an afternoon task, done in an unusual manner, where all of us would sit together on two sides of a long table in the common sign- out room. Whenever there was an interesting case, the slides would be passed around for everyone's opinion.

The same was done whenever there was any doubt about the right diagnosis. I did not notice any sense of embarrassment from anyone asking for help nor did I notice any bruised ego when a diagnosis was challenged. Doing this each day made me realize that this was a wonderful way to learn from the chief, who was almost always present during these sign outs, and from each other. It was also a venue in which each of us got to know the diagnoses of the interesting cases each day and, therefore, was able to answer queries from surgeons, whom we happened to bump into in the corridors, at lunch, or at a coffee break, saving them precious time in trying to find someone who could give them the information they were seeking. As I wove myself into the fabric of the department, I soon learned that trust was the coin of the realm, the foundation on which we built our careers.

We pathologists are often referred to as "a doctor's doctor" simply because much of our work involved supplying doctors with test results and diagnoses on which they have to rely on for their practice.

In particular, the surgeons, our biggest client pool in surgical pathology, were the most vulnerable in their reliance on our diagnostic acumen, especially in the area of frozen sections where an error might not only cost the patient a needless loss of an organ, but might also involve the surgeon and us in a nasty lawsuit.

In my opinion, frozen sections were where pathologists earned their pay, where indecisions, if ever exhibited, were at times interpreted as a sure sign of incompetency and where no margin of error was allowed.

I experienced my share of distrust. Within the first few months in my new environment, I was called to do many frozen sections, and each time I did one where my diagnosis would necessitate a change in the surgeon's plan of action, I would hear "Could you ask Henry to have a look?" Henry would dutifully appear and look and chide them with remarks like "You didn't have to call me you know. She is quite qualified." or "My diagnosis is the same as hers. You really don't need me."

Henry's consistent polite repudiation of a surgeon's lack of trust in me was invaluable to me as a morale booster, and I was very grateful for his unflagging support.

Gradually, the request for Henry's second opinion diminished and the OR became more friendly. One anesthetist began to call me "love," and one surgeon would always greet me with "Emmy baby, how are you?" Then one day, confronted with a diagnostic puzzle on frozen section, I went into the OR and said, "Sorry, guys, I don't know what it is. You'll have to close up and wait for the permanent sections." The surgeon looked at me and said, "Will do." With that, I felt that I had finally "arrived" in earning their trust. All of them except for one particular surgeon, Sam.

Sam would always say "Is this Henry's diagnosis too?" whenever I called him in the late afternoon to inform him of a diagnosis other than what he thought clinically. Sam would also accost me in the morning when he saw me coming in to work at an hour, he felt was late and would look at his watch and remark, "Banker's hours, huh?" At surgical conferences, he would go out of his way to dispute my opinion.

And, of course, at every frozen section he requested that I happened to do, he would ask for Henry's second opinion. This went on for a year with no let up and with me essentially allowing him to continue, until one morning I saw him coming toward me as I emerged from the parking garage. I cringed inwardly, preparing myself for another unpleasant encounter, because I was definitely not in the mood for it that particular morning.

He stopped in front of me and said with a sneer, "I suppose you are late because you had to make the beds, feed the kids, and make lunch for your husband." I answered back in a voice filled with irritation that I had suppressed for so long and said, "Yes, I did, and I would like you to know that my contract allows me to do all that."

He looked genuinely surprised as I left him standing by the sidewalk.

Still angry, I marched into Henry's office and said, "What is it about Sam that he has to be so nasty towards me all the time?"

Henry answered with a sigh, "Sam hates females, foreigners, and hospital-based physicians. And you are all three. But just to let you know that he doesn't discriminate, he tried to block my nomination to be president of the medical staff on the basis that I'm a hospital-based physician, which to him disqualified me because he views us as 'parasites' with no patients of our own."

What a jerk, I thought. But even jerks deserve a reconsideration of their special status in society.

Sam immediately stopped his badgering. No longer did he ask for a second opinion on my diagnoses. No longer did he make sneering remarks when he met me. Most surprisingly, he came to visit me in my office one day, chatting with me about our families during which time he revealed to me that he never got over the death of his oldest son who died in a motorcycle accident, a piece of news that not even Henry, who had been in the same hospital with Sam for a quarter of a century, knew.

I was truly puzzled by the entire episode with Sam. I asked myself what did this all mean? I juggled with a few probabilities. Was he just a nasty person, happy to torment someone because he could? Was he just expressing his dislike of what I represented, a female foreigner hospital-based physician, or was he just testing me all this time to see when I would stand up to him?

After much thought, I finally concluded that it was probably all three. I certainly had no control over the first two reasons, but the third offered me a good lesson to learn.

I resolved then that I would never tolerate this kind of treatment again. I would address it right away. But as is often said, resolutions are made to be broken.

Batting down one's peers is one thing, but trying to combat the chief of surgery was another. Paul was no doubt the smartest and best-known surgeon who practiced on the North Shore. He was reputed to be the best surgical resident ever produced by the Massachusetts General Hospital's surgical program. After his residency, he dwelled within the midst of rarified milieu of academia, where he became very quickly very prominent. He developed such high esteem within the surgical community that he was rumored to be on the short list of candidates for the position of surgeon-in-chief for the Peter Bent Brigham Hospital. He would have been the youngest person ever to be considered for that post, but unfortunately, he failed to get the appointment.

Unaccustomed to losing, Paul decided to spurn his former life to go into private practice and settled on the North Shore, attracted no doubt by the many beautiful residential areas along the ocean. He soon established a booming practice and was the chief of surgery when I arrived.

Due to his keen intellect and his years in academia, he was still the professor and everyone else were students. Soon after my appointment to the department, the secretary received a call from the operating room. Paul needed "the girl" for a frozen section. It took the secretary a while to realize that I was "the girl."

I went into the operating room where he handed me half a nodular thyroid gland and said, "Give me three differential diagnoses." I was a little taken aback by this. What did he think I was? Was I, as Guillermo had once answered an arrogant surgeon, a correspondence school graduate?

I didn't want to make a scene as there were surgical residents, student nurses, and physicians in the room, all seemingly waiting for an answer from me. So I gave him the answers he wanted and left to do the frozen section. I decided to give Paul the benefit of the doubt. Perhaps he wasn't trying to demean me. After all, we were a teaching hospital with residents in many of the services and he had every right to exercise his role as a teacher. Appointing me as "the girl," Paul decided to call Matt "the boy" and began grilling Matt in the OR in the same way. Matt did not take to this kindly and swore to me that he would pay Paul back.

Our surgical residents were from Massachusetts General Hospital, affectionately known as "the Fruit Street Clinic." The residents and Paul met with us every Wednesday noon to review all the specimens they had removed during the previous week, both grossly and microscopically. The purpose of these meetings was to teach the residents surgical pathology, and these sessions brought forth all of Paul's professorial flair. He would try his utmost to impress everyone that he was as good a pathologist as he was a surgeon. I always felt I had to be on my toes, anticipating his questions.

One Wednesday, Matt said he would like to present a special case just for Paul to diagnose since he was such a good pathologist. He projected a photo of a piece of skin with a black lesion on it. Paul studied it and gave one diagnosis after another without satisfying Matt. I could see he was getting annoyed and embarrassed in front of his residents, and I was starting to get an uncomfortable feeling that this was Matt's revenge.

Finally, Paul gave up, and Matt said, "Fooled you."

Matt had taken a piece of normal skin and drew a lesion on it with ink. Paul stopped quizzing us in the OR.

It was the summer of my third year when disaster struck.

Two years previously, Lewis and his family went to Mexico for their vacation, where he contracted an unknown disorder characterized by low-grade fever and a widened mediastinum (midportion of the chest) on X-ray, thought to be due to enlarged lymph nodes. His own diagnosis was Hodgkin's disease, which appeared to correspond to what he had, mainly enlarged lymph nodes and at times accompanied by low-grade fever. His internist did not think it was Hodgkin's but had no name for his illness. Over a period of a year, his fever and the abnormality noted in his chest disappeared.

For his vacation this year, he decided to go to Puerto Rico with his family. He had barely arrived in Puerto Rico when he was struck down by a massive heart attack. His blood samples were sent to us for testing because we had the fastest machine to do it. His cardiac enzymes were off the chart.

Lewis recuperated for a while in Puerto Rico, returned when able, and stayed home until he was ready to return to work. While he was still recovering, Matt and a chemistry tech contracted hepatitis B at the same time. The co-incident was traced to their standing together alongside an open spinning centrifuge containing test tubes with blood of patients infected with hepatitis B. Being a bachelor, Matt went home to Syracuse so his mother could take care of him.

Before this incident, Matt confided in me that he was seriously thinking of leaving us. He was in negotiation with a pathologist who offered him a two-year period on salary followed by full partnership. He was one of the new age pathologists who firmly believed in equality in the work place, and he saw no chance of that happening with our setup where Henry had the contract with the hospital and we were Henry's employees.

Lewis in the meantime came back to work part-time. He was profoundly changed. He refused to do any autopsies. He was very often impatient as if he was parceling out precious time that he didn't have. Very often, he seemed lost in thoughts when we were in conversation.

I attributed these changes to his need for time to cope with the aftermath of a life-threatening illness. Time passed, and he seemed to regain his balance so much so that our group met, without Matt but with Lewis's radiologist friends, for dinner at a Chinese restaurant on the night of the moon landing. All the diners in the restaurant watched with awe and fascination. He seemed to be almost normal, and we all left the restaurant in a happy mood.

A few weeks later, as I passed by his office, he beckoned me cheerfully into his office to show me a hemoglobinometer that he was evaluating for our use. He patiently explained to me his methodology and showed me the notebook with his recordings. I was mystified as to why he was doing this since he had never shown me any of his evaluations before. I thanked him and went about with my own chores. In the early afternoon of that day, I saw Lewis leaving. He paused at the receptionist's desk and had a few words with her. I heard them both laugh. When I passed by the same area, the receptionist remarked to me how well Lewis looked and how cheerful he was and that he was leaving early to have his checkup by his internist.

Lewis had left for the parking lot, got into his car, and started the engine. A nurse entering the lot waited for him to pull out so she could park in his place, but when Lewis failed to back out, she parked somewhere else. On her way out of the lot, she headed to Lewis' car to tease him about his sluggishness in vacating that spot. That's when she found him slumped over his steering wheel.

The emergency room physicians tried for two hours to revive him without success. The department was stunned by the loss. He was in his forties.

Lewis's duties fell on me like a ton of bricks, and I was totally unprepared. In a very, very short period, I had to learn to deal with techs from all sections in the lab, trying to answer the myriad questions that needed answers. I was called to fix malfunctioning equipment that I knew very little about because Lewis always did that. We had no maintenance contract for any of the equipment. I was bombarded by salesmen who came to tell me all the equipment Lewis had ordered, which I had no way of knowing whether it was true or not.

At the same time, I was doing all the autopsies and much of the surgicals even though Henry was doing as much as he could. I had no time for nuclear medicine and had to leave the department for Jack to handle.

During the few minutes we were free to talk to each other, I told Henry of Matt's plan to leave us and his reasons. Henry asked me to call Matt, who was still at home, to ask him not to leave. I was also asked to assure him that he, Henry, would "open up the books" to Matt's demand for equal pay.

I was by now working twelve to fourteen hours daily, and Matt's return was something I desperately wanted. I called Matt and conveyed

Henry's message and begged him to stay. Matt declined the offer because he was not convinced that Henry would do what he said.

He did however return for a period, helping us tremendously while Henry furiously interviewed candidate after candidate.

I moved into Lewis's office from a chair in the resident's room. For the first time I looked in his file cabinet and was astounded to find the amount of literature on Hodgkin's disease. He also had a very up-to-date collection of articles in hematology, an area that he was particularly interested in.

Henry and I struggled daily to get the work done. One day, he and I decided to take time out to make a general assessment of what changes we needed to make in the aftermath of Lewis's death. We purchased maintenance contracts immediately for all our instruments. We reviewed whether we had adequate supervision for each section in the lab. We had a very good man with a master's degree supervising microbiology and a very capable tech specialist in blood banking to care for that section. Henry asked me to take charge of hematology and appointed me the director of nuclear medicine. We decided that both of us would temporarily take care of chemistry. After interviewing dozens of candidates, Henry finally settled on Alex as our new colleague. He was more of a clinical than an anatomic pathologist, a fit for our needs. Lucky for us too, he was interested in blood banking and he was quite capable of supervising chemistry.

Henry also in quick succession hired Alkam, my old fellow trainee from my Children's Hospital days, to shore up our AP (anatomic pathology) needs. With our new responsibilities in place, we attempted to move forward with a unified purpose.

But trouble brewed in my absence in nuclear medicine. Jack, who was left in charge, wanted to take over the department. Rumors appeared that he actually started the department and that we were the intruders, which was truly ridiculous, considering the fact that nuclear medicine was within the physical makeup of our department and that it was hard to believe that anything belonging to radiology would ever be situated anywhere but within the confines of radiology. Relationship between the two departments had always been extremely friendly, due to Lewis's efforts, but was now palpably frosty.

I finally complained to Henry that we needed to do something.

Henry, the epitome of a gentleman, did not want any trouble with the radiology department. He met with the chief of radiology and proposed a co- directorship for nuclear medicine, with me from our side and Hubie, a new radiologist, also interested in nuclear medicine, from their side. The two chiefs agreed with this new setup for the department, and a new beginning ensued.

I was at this time pregnant with our third child. This time, six weeks before the due date, I felt the first pangs of the oncoming delivery just before a conference I was about to conduct. I quickly asked Alkam to take over and left for the delivery room.

As with my previous pregnancies, I worked until it was time for delivery. At each pregnancy, I would warn the obstetrician not to give me Demerol because of the bad reaction I experienced with the first delivery, but in haste, this was forgotten. The obstetrician in my second pregnancy was finishing his rounds, and the birthing process went faster than thought. With any delivery becoming imminent, doctors would give Demerol almost automatically which I got again. This, of course, brought on the expected reaction and resulted in profuse apologies from everyone involved.

This time a premature baby girl was delivered without Demerol, who promptly turned as yellow as a canary. Wearing eye pads, she was placed under a lamp within an incubator, and when her siblings first saw her, the oldest, then six years old, said "Can we return her?"

I came back to work after the fifth day and made "bilirubin" rounds on the new baby every day until it dropped to normal, and she was allowed to leave for home. To show how crazily competitive some of us are, on the day I returned for work, I was stopped in the corridor by Glen, a radiologist who had just had his stomach partially removed due to a bleeding ulcer. He asked, "How many days?"

"Five," I answered.

"Phew, I'm still the winner." He had returned to work four days after his operation. He was the most macho of the radiologists, and he would definitely not be able to tolerate a woman beating him in any way. In fact, he had the personality of a surgeon and was training to be one when his gastric ulcer forced him to change his career choice.

He was known to the medical staff as someone who was "never wrong," the type who refused to recognize facts because they were so convinced of their own infallibility. Every hospital had one or two of those. Glen was not beloved either by his often-inappropriate remarks such as the one made to a cafeteria worker about her colonoscopy result when she was serving food to him in the cafeteria line.

He also informed me in the presence of many male colleagues during a coffee break that my mammography was hard to read because my breasts were "too small and dense." So, I was a bit surprised to see he had a kind and solicitous side to him when he asked me, after Henry hired Alex for our department, "Are you being paid enough?"

Although I said, "I am," I really had no idea. I had accepted the fact that Alex would no doubt be paid more than me.

When Henry hired me, I didn't have a ready answer when he asked about my salary expectations. He then asked me what I was making, and when I answered, I sold myself short a thousand dollars by not remembering that I was going to get a raise. Being an experienced person in the area of hiring, Henry offered me a thousand more than what I was making. Now, almost three years later, he had nearly tripled my salary for which I was indeed very appreciative and it would not allow me in good conscience to complain. In fact, in all the years I worked for Henry, I never asked for nor disputed the amount of money he allotted me each year. It was his custom at the start of each year to see me privately and tell what my salary was going to be. And each year, I would say "Thank you." I trusted him to give me my fair share.

With Alex and Alkam in place, we looked to expand our horizons collectively. One of the first area of our expansion occurred by chance. Henry happened to be in the comptroller's office one day and happened to ask him what the hospital's collection was on the cytologies (basically Pap smears) we were doing for the OB-GYN physicians. To his surprise, the answer was "about 10 percent."

"Why?" asked Henry.

"No idea," was the answer.

Henry though had a very good idea why. He had surmised that a patient would go to Dr. X who did the Pap smear and who then would send it to us for diagnosis. Since the hospital billed for our work, it would then send the patient a bill and the patient would look at the bill and say, "This must be a mistake because I never went to the hospital," and would most likely throw the bill away.

Henry shared that information with us. Alex had a very good business sense and immediately advised, "We should take over the billing." Henry negotiated the takeover, and we bought space in the new medical building across the hospital to do the work privately under the auspices of this new private laboratory. The very first return from the billing for the cytology was 95 percent. All we did was add a line in our bill, "Your doctor has sent your Pap smear to us for interpretation."

This single endeavor of diagnosing Pap smears grew into a full-fledged private pathology lab where surgicals and clinical pathology services became available to the doctor's offices bringing profits to Henry, Alex, and me. The advent of Medicare affected how pathologists were paid. This transformed us from hospital-paid pathologists to physicians who could bill the insurance companies, including Medicare Part B for surgical pathology. Payments for lab tests to pathologists were much debated until it was decided by law that the hospital would pay the pathologists a set amount through Medicare Part A for the supervision of the clinical lab instead of payments for individual tests to pathologists.

Changes within our department were also taking place. The chemistry department now had a PhD supervising it. Students in medical technology from a university in Boston rotated through our lab, and we had a medical technology coordinator taking full-time care of these students. We also had our own AP resident and a CP resident, Dave, from another university hospital in Boston.

The fact that we were a teaching hospital and we had our own pathology residency program prompted the pathology department of the medical center to discuss with us about having a conjoint residency program where the AP residents from the medical center would do their CP residency at our hospital. This would enable the medical center to offer an AP/CP training program, which most trainees in pathology now demanded.

The official organization concerned with residency education approved this conjoint entity and soon our department saw the addition of two CP residents and one AP resident from the medical center.

Although all of us took part in "educating" them, the overall job of taking care of them fell on my shoulders. The residents were all very smart, and a few were super smart. I struggled to be one step ahead of them while the PhD chemist fell three steps behind. This elicited unkind remarks regarding his competency. To avoid being targeted the same way by the residents, I felt an urgent need to have the necessary credentials. I needed to be certified by the Board of Pathology in Clinical Pathology. I had only an anatomic pathology certification.

Since Dave, our rotating CP resident, was preparing for his AP/CP board exams, I decided to team up with him to study. For preparation, I would jot down notes on index cards (textbooks were too heavy to tote around) and carried these cards everywhere I went, reviewing the notes while waiting to pick up my children after lessons or birthday parties or standing in line for food in the cafeteria. At times, the task to master the topics appeared hopeless.

My partnership in learning with Dave was an unforgettable experience.

Dave met me each weekend at the Lexington Library with his car trunk filled with books, a traveling reference library. We devoted most of our time to CP subjects since it was so widespread and difficult to master. We would quiz each other as we studied, and each time Dave failed to give a correct answer, he would fly into a rage, cursing the Board of Pathology for making him take this exam. He would simultaneously vow to kill himself and/or the board members if he failed. He would rant that he was devoting precious time for this stupid exam while his two-year-old child was growing up deprived of his loving attention. I knew how he felt. I was doing the same with my own children, but I did not possess the passion to kill anyone.

At the end of each session, we would go over a stack of previous test questions compiled by conscientious candidates who had taken the test before us. This was one of the most helpful guide available for our preparation. We continued our studies until the three-day examination, one and a half day each for the AP and CP, to be held in Florida that year. Dave was there ahead of me because the AP exam was given first. On the day of my test, I went to the site a little ahead of the start of the examination and the first person I met in the lobby was Dave and he was beside himself. He had failed to identify the sixth characteristic in a syndrome we had reviewed. He ushered me to his hotel room where I noted that his traveling library was now piled on the second bed. I tried hard to calm him down and told him that I was certain that he would pass. I reminded him that he still had another day and a half of tests to take and that he couldn't afford to waste his energies on negative thoughts. We proceeded to the examination together. As I predicted, he passed and so did I.

We had some wonderful people passing through our conjoint residency program, including many women whose presence I enjoyed immensely. For the first time, I got a chance to guide, encourage, and make friends with female physicians, a totally different experience from my past.

Unfortunately, we also had a few terrible trainees who should have never been in pathology and should have been cut from the program.

By now, Dr. Mann had retired. We gave him a warm send-off party in one of the best restaurants in town, and he honored us by becoming our consultant visiting us once a week. In particular, after all these years, he chose to reward me by giving me a signed photograph of himself.

The new crew at the medical center was of a different sort entirely. The pathologist-in-chief was not even a pathologist. Although all of us continued to teach at the medical school and were promoted regularly until both Alex and I became clinical professors, teaching became a burden. We no longer had our own set of students throughout the year because the school felt it was unfair for the students to be stuck with a "poor" teacher for a year. Instead, the students were rotated from instructor to instructor every few weeks. The time allotted with the students was also reduced from two hours to one, and by the time the session got going, we had about forty-five minutes to do our job. My commute from home to school in rush hour traffic was about an hour and the return trip to the hospital was close to half an hour. I had very little satisfaction with this task.

Still, after twenty-five years of teaching, the medical school decided to honor us at a tea ceremony where each one of us was given a watch with the school insignia forming the face of the watch. With great embarrassment, the school had to return the watch presented to me in exchange for a woman's model. You would think that after twenty-five years, they would have noticed that I was a woman.

Alex now had a lot of time on his hand because chemistry was ably supervised. He and Henry began to investigate the possibility of computerizing our lab, and this project took both of them away often, evaluating all the existing systems not only at the companies manufacturing these systems but also at the various large labs that had some of these systems. After deciding to get the Digital Equipment Corporation's PDP system, Henry had to convince the board of directors of the hospital to put up the money for the purchase. It was not an easy sell due to the large amount of money involved, but he was able to convince them that computerization of lab data was the way of the future and the acquisition would make us way ahead of every community hospital not only on the North Shore but in the Commonwealth.

The adaptation of lab data to the computerized format that we wanted and also readily accepted by the clinicians took a long time.

Up until the computer's presence, lab data were written by hand onto preprinted slips, different sections of which were identified by different colors bordering the slip, such as red borders for hematology, yellow for urine results, blue for chemistry, etc.

These slips were then affixed to designated lab sheets (hematology, urine, chemistry, etc.) enabling physicians to review them in a manner that allowed them to detect changes in the results on a daily basis. To present the same data in a computerized form needed input from the users so each group of doctors were asked to weigh in on how they wanted data such as hematology and chemistry values to appear in computer printouts.

After numerous meetings, an agreement was reached and a defined form emerged suitable to our medical staff. Little by little, the clinicians adapted themselves to the new format of lab data and in private conservations with us would divulge that they loved it.

But very simple tasks took ages to resolve. For example, new data on every patient was printed every day and distributed to the floors and despite the fact that we met with all the nurses on every shift to teach them where they should put the new data sheet so that the doctors would see the new data first, loads of complaints poured in about misplaced sheets. It occurred so often that we finally decided to have a lab person go to each floor each day to place them correctly in each patient's chart.

After handling and solving most of the problems presented by our attempt to modernize, Alex imparted a distinct impression to the medical staff that he was the lab's computer guru.

Alex also convinced Henry that he should be an active player in the College of American Pathologists (CAP), a body devoted to the well-being of pathology and the practicing pathologist. With Henry's blessing, he soon became the treasurer of the organization. This took a great deal of his time, which included frequent travels to Chicago for meetings. He also enrolled himself in an MBA program out of Colorado, which took more of his time. In fact, he became so busy that it became his practice to hand us his "outside" schedule for us to work around. We got so used to his frequent absence in our daily activities that none of us bothered to complain, even behind his back.

Nuclear medicine, as expected, matured into a specialty with a Board of Nuclear Medicine formed to certify candidates who would fulfill a required two-year training program. For those of us practicing the science without formal training, the board issued a "grandfather" clause which permitted us to take the first examination given by the board. Both Alex and I decided to formalize our credentials and plunged into studying for the exam. Luckily, both of us became certified.

The stewardship of nuclear medicine by Hubie and me progressed smoothly. He was a very likable, laid-back person, easy to work with.

With the computer installed and working in the lab, Hubie and I decided to do the same for nuclear medicine. Thus far, the scans produced were static studies. We would inject the isotopes for bones, liver, brain, etc. and record these areas on film for us to diagnose. With the availability of thallium, we became the first to provide scanning of the heart muscles for damage. This particular test whetted our appetite for expansion from static studies to dynamic blood flow studies that would allow us to calculate ejection fractions of the heart, renal filtration rate, and even identification of bleeding sites within the gastrointestinal tract.

What we needed was the right computer system. Again, this process took time. After evaluating all the available systems on the market, we settled on a French system Informatek. Not only was the hardware suitable for our needs, the company also furnished us an in-house brilliant programmer named Elizabeth, who wrote programs to our specifications.

When all the software was in place, we asked for volunteers to establish normal baselines. Then we teamed up with a cardiologist for a double-blind study on cardiac ejection fractions, a test which determines whether a heart's pumping action is normal or not. We asked this cardiologist to continue to send his patient not only to Massachusetts General Hospital but also to us to compare results. After a series of patients, our results turned out to be the same as Mass. General. The data were presented to the medical staff, and since our procedures was much less invasive, all the cardiologists began to send their patients to us.

We now entered the best and exciting period of innovative testing in nuclear medicine with the aid of a computer.

Although all our departments were functioning at peak efficiency, the winds of change were blowing through the structural foundation of all hospitals.

When I joined the hospital, there were three administrators: the director, the assistant director, and the director of nursing.

The requests for any particular need of the department went straight to the top. If the director was absent, the assistant took care of it. The director of nursing took care of nursing problems.

Now hospitals decided that they needed to be more like a corporation.

Acting like a corporation enabled the hospital to expand, taking advantage of new business opportunities in healthcare. It would allow the new entity to "streamline" its accounting system in a linear manner to save money, and best of all for the corporation, it would change the traditional way in which hospital workers would be controlled.

Also, as a corporation, profit would be put before service and mission.

Soon the hospital's director became president and with that came loads of vice-presidents— for human resources, clinical services, nursing services, financial services, and so on down the line.

For the laboratory, our traditional chief technologist was renamed as an administrative director of laboratory who was given the power to evaluate, hire, and fire techs and who would no longer answer to us, the pathologists, but to the vice-president of clinical services. With this change, the pathologist's relationship to the technologists was irrevocably altered. We were no longer in charge of them. They were no longer beholden to us for their jobs. In fact, we were totally out of the loop in the everyday management of the lab.

This reorganization of hospital administration made life so much easier for the administrator in charge of the laboratory. He now dealt with a subordinate rather than with the pathologists, and orders given by him to cut our staff over and over again were carried out obediently with little argument from our new administrative director. Complaints from the pathologists, on the other hand, took ages to reach the appropriate person, with little or no response.

Changes were also stirring within the pathology department. At this juncture, our microbiology supervisor decided to leave. This was an important area that held no interest nor expertise among us. At the same time, Alkam also decided to leave. With these two impending departures, the logical solution was to find a pathologist with an interest in microbiology.

We ran through our list of former residents and pinpointed Butto, who was now a staff pathologist at a Harvard teaching hospital. Unbeknownst to all of us, Butto was having a bad week. He had always thought that he was the heir apparent to the chief of the department of microbiology, who was rumored to be retiring. His impression was further bolstered by the fact that the hospital sent him to Mayo Clinic for a comprehensive course on virology for the purpose of starting a new virology service. While there, someone casually mentioned to him that his hospital had just named a new chief of microbiology, which stunned him. When he returned, he found an impersonal note on his desk informing him of this appointment.

Butto, a former resident whom we became well-acquainted, was an extremely smart person from Pakistan, where he had attended medical school as a presidential scholar. His particular interest in microbiology suited us perfectly.

I called him and induced him with higher pay, working with people whom he knew well, and Henry's promise of future partnership in our private lab. He joined us. We were back to full staff and coverage for all departments.

Alex in the meantime was scanning the horizon to expand our services to pathology departments in other hospitals. He was worried how our hospital was faring. We had changed presidents, the hospital was losing money, and the hospital also had not quite recovered from a crippling nurse's strike, which fractured the relationship between doctors and nurses.

In quick succession, Alex secured contracts to service the pathology department of a neighboring hospital and to head the department of clinical pathology, but not the anatomic pathology section, of a university hospital in Boston. The position required someone special, someone like Alex who had the credential of a Harvard Medical School graduate with an MBA, AP, CP, and nuclear medicine certification and subspecialty certifications in blood banking and dermatopathology. In reality, Alex was really whom they wanted. He was also the best politician among us and, therefore, would be capable of navigating the tricky course of politics in academia.

The commute though from the North Shore, where he lived, to Boston was a killer.

In our general effort to expand our services, we managed to get ourselves appointed by the governor of Massachusetts, Governor Michael Dukakis, as state pathologists to help do autopsies on state forensic cases other than homicides.

For many, many years, Massachusetts had not been able to attract anyone to fill the job of chief medical examiner due to the fact that the salary offered was insulting. After many publicized mishandlings of cases, the politicians finally decided to offer the job with a decent salary, which also carried an academic appointment from the University of Massachusetts Medical School to garner additional income. Special permission to do private consulting was also granted.

These provisions enabled the state to capture one of the best chief medical examiners the state has ever had. This chief remained for several years, providing us with guidance for our difficult cases and preparing us thoroughly for occasional court appearances. We were all very sorry to see him leave. It was also during this period that pathologists in Massachusetts realized collectively the tremendous number of specimens sent by us to the referral labs all around the country. Together, we met and planned to establish our own reference lab with every willing pathologist contributing five thousand dollars to this cause. The contributions elicited enabled us to start off modestly. We hired a PhD to manage this lab, and over time, this entity grew in size and scope, collecting specimens from all over Massachusetts and from neighboring states as well.

I was elected to be one of the board of directors and sat through a turbulent period during which the PhD director had to be replaced due to psychotic behavior, where pickup of specimens from out-of-state became a losing proposition, and where the financial state of the lab became more and more precarious due to changes pressed upon private practitioners from the hospitals with which they were affiliated. These hospitals were directly in competition with us for the specimens originating from physician offices.

Our reference lab by this time was closely allied with Mayo Clinic, which did much of our esoteric tests, and our relationship with them was such that they soon took over the operation. None of us got back the money we invested.

Our hospital, like many others, was caught in the throes of convulsive changes. A new president named Mullen appeared. The story about him was that he was a failed banker who happened to be a close friend of the chairman of the board of directors of the hospital. He was supposed to be a sham president, only for show, a save-face offer handed to him from a friend when he failed to be promoted to the presidency of his bank. When he was appointed, those under him understood that they would continue to run the institution without his interference. This appointment turned out to be a disaster of such magnitude that it changed the course of all our lives.

Mullen soon fired everyone who knew how to run a hospital. He decided to install a new computer system for billing. Rumors had it that he chose a particular computer company because many of the board directors of the hospital owned stock in the company. Rumors also had it that the billing system was in such a mess that it did not send out any bill for a long, long time.

Soon the hospital was hemorrhaging money. The medical staff was in revolt, and once, during a tumultuous medical meeting where we first voted no-confidence in Mullen, a well-respected surgeon stood up and said to Mullen's face, "When you took over, you were supposed to direct the bus. Now you are driving it and killing everyone in it."

Another vote of no-confidence was repeated soon after, but the medical staff's public display of contempt for Mullen failed to activate any response from the board.

Hospitals all around us by now were closing or merging. Our genius of a president decided to join the trend. The city we were in had a larger hospital (us) and a smaller hospital (them) within a couple of miles from each other. Many of our staff members were on staff in both places, but few of them were on the staff of our hospital. No rivalry existed between us. We felt superior; they didn't feel inferior. The two hospitals and their staff coexisted cordially.

Whatever transpired behind the scenes, the boards of directors from both hospitals convinced themselves that we should merge. A heavyweight consulting firm was hired to assess this possibility and teach us how to do this.

Swarms of young MBAs with their clipboards invaded every corner of the hospital, scribbling their findings, which resulted in a report that advised us to merge because the city no longer needed two hospitals and that we, the larger hospital, should move to the smaller hospital due to its newer facilities.

The staff immediately reacted. Large numbers of our best physicians moved to another hospital in an adjacent city, taking with them all their patients.

During this turmoil, with the hospital so vulnerable, the cardiologists decided to challenge the department of nuclear medicine's right to do cardiac studies. They threatened to leave en masse unless given the right to take over that part of our department. The entire maneuver was obviously financially motivated.

The cardiologists envisioned ordering these procedures on their patients and getting paid for supervising the tests and for interpreting the results. The hospital could not afford to lose the cardiologists and all their patients.

It didn't matter to the administrators who did the work, and no one cared to even bring up the issue of conflict of interest with the cardiologists who would be ordering and charging for these procedures, as well as getting paid additionally for interpreting the results. Transferring that part of our department to the cardiologists felt like a kick in the gut. We had no recourse but to surrender what we felt was the best and most interesting part of our work. Only one cardiologist, the very first one who started with us on this new adventure, came to express his regrets to me.

Reluctantly, we all began to prepare for the eventual merge of the two hospitals. The two departments of pathology planned coordinated conferences and meetings to feel comfortable with each other. This was not an easy task since Koop, a Massachusetts General Hospital-trained, long-time chief of pathology at the smaller hospital, harbored a distinct dislike for Henry, even though Henry was withdrawing from his leadership role and letting Alex take over. This natural progression on our side led us to the thorny question of who was going to be the new chief when we merged. At this stage in the merger, any advantage for one side was taken as an affront by the other.

Koop had an associate whom I had introduced to him, a father of one of my daughter's classmates, which turned into a total fiasco.

He was once an academic pathologist at the hospital of an Ivy League university and possessed a long list of published articles. He and his family moved to Andover because their oldest son was enrolled at Andover. The younger daughters went to a private primary school where my daughters were attending too.

When my youngest daughter was invited to their house, she would come back and report that neither the father nor the mother of her friend worked. When another curious parent told me that she had seen a letter addressed to them as Dr. and Dr., I assumed that they were researchers who did their work at home and gave no more thought to it until one day my daughter's friend was brought to our house by her father, who asked me in a nonchalant way, "How is the market in pathology?" Totally surprised, I asked, "Are you a pathologist?" When he answered in the affirmative, I told him that Koop was looking for one. I was not surprised that he got the job. What did surprise me was his irresponsible behavior.

When we had our meetings, and we found that he didn't do what he was supposed to do, he would excuse himself by saying, "I'm not paid enough to do this." He displayed no embarrassment when he repeated the same statement over and over for other neglected duties.

This particular attitude prompted me to suggest to Alex that when we merged we should do it as equals, salary wise, so no one could complain of being treated differently. Despite Alex's vigorous objections, we did do that but that didn't get our "I'm not paid enough" associate to act differently.

The thorny question of who would be the new chief came up shortly after the two departments merged. Koop actually nominated me to be the new chief, but I declined. I was not meant to be chief of a department, going to meetings, spending time on administrative duties, and dealing with the administration. I preferred doing the work.

This difficult decision was tabled for a while, but we eventually voted for Alex. It was a bitter pill for Koop to swallow, but we outnumbered him four to two.

While the merger among the pathologists was not easy, merging our technical staff was not easy either. Seniority had to be determined, resulting in many layoffs. Accusations of favoritism for one side, which was at the same time interpreted as animosity for the other side, were constantly thrown at us. Amid all the chaos involved in a merger, the administration renamed the two merged hospitals with a grandiose name suggesting that we gave care to the entire Atlantic coast. It was rumored that the logo designed cost us a tidy sum of $60,000—money we could ill afford.

During this time Alex struggled daily with the commute to Boston, trying his best to utilize the time spent in traffic tie-ups by calling us daily by phone to discuss our mutual concerns. He was encountering problems in his job.

His aggressive personality produced paranoia from the chief of the anatomic pathology division who was deathly afraid that Alex was scheming to take over that part of the department. This paranoia generated multidirectional arrows of criticisms aimed at Alex with increasing frequency that even Alex found it hard to bear.

Besides, the commute was killing him. He wanted out as soon as possible, and we agreed to his request. In his preparation to leave Boston, Alex discovered two hospitals seeking pathologists to staff their departments, prompting him to pursue these openings with all his energy.

One of the two hospitals had a reputation of being waspish, staffed with men of the old order, the kind perceived to be uncomfortable with women or foreign-trained physicians. We discussed this perceived problem at length. Finally, Alex decided to bring Koop's associate, a white male, to the meeting with the governing members of the hospital for the critical interview instead of me.

We later learned that at the interview, Alex did most of the talking but one member, trying to engage Koop's associate, asked, "Are you in charge of microbiology?" The answer was, "I don't know shit about microbiology." Alex nearly fell off his seat. He knew instantly that we were not going to be their first choice to take over their department. Because Alex knew the chairman of this committee, he managed to secure a second interview where I was asked to go with him. We did our best, but we knew this was going to be an uphill struggle, confirmed by the fact that two members did not even bother to show up. Although the interviewers relayed positive impressions to Alex, we failed to correct the damage done. This was a great loss for us due partly to our own biased decision. We incorrectly assumed the interviewer's reception of a foreign-trained female physician was going to be negative. We didn't know how to fire a colleague, but he saved us that ordeal by leaving us soon after.

We were luckier with the second hospital. This hospital had their pathology department serviced by a nearby university-affiliated hospital. The medical staff was not happy with the arrangement because they felt that their coverage was generally assigned to "junior" members of the mother hospital with resultant diagnoses unduly delayed due to their inexperience.

Armed with this information, Alex spent long hours wooing the administration and meeting with influential physicians of that hospital to persuade them to recommend us to take over the pathology department. We succeeded only because of the hard work and time put in by Alex. Once this tough job of negotiation was done, Alex left Boston. With him came two young pathologists who wanted to join us. One was a genius of a sort, graduating from MIT with a patent to his name. He was also a whiz in chemistry. Even though he was trained at one of the best hospitals in town in anatomic pathology, his former department chief endorsed him by telling us that he would not let Harry near a surgical specimen with a ten-foot pole.

The other pathologist was DeeDee, another impeccably trained pathologist who had spent the last eight years of her professional life in blood banking. Although they were not a good fit for us, we took them, putting Harry in charge of chemistry and allowing DeeDee to catch up on her surgical pathology skills.

A year later, Harry left to work for a large commercial laboratory with a big chemistry section. DeeDee was assigned with Alex to staff our newest acquisition. When we first took over this new department, the number of surgical specimens was pitifully low, numbering in the three thousand for a hospital with close to two hundred beds. In less than five years, we built the surgical number to over eight thousand.

Back at home base, unhappy with the upheaval produced by the move of the larger hospital to the smaller one, the administration decided to hire the same consultants to assess and advise us about the state of our merger. To everyone's surprise, the consultants wanted us to move back to the larger hospital. This decision brought the same revolt within the staff of the smaller hospital, and like the previous exodus of the larger hospital's staff, half of them left in disgust to the same neighboring hospital, also taking their patients with them.

The existing sentiment among the staff of the smaller hospital regarding the consultant's suggestion was expressed by a surgeon whom I had known since he was a medical student working in the lab of my former hospital.

"So, we are now going to be moved to the shithouse," he fumed.

I was so offended by his remark that I asked him, "So you think we are all shit?"

The move never took place. We were all too exhausted with anger, disgust, and disbelief that the administration could be so incompetent. The larger hospital, our hospital, a hospital that had served the city for over a hundred years was eventually phased out and imploded, leaving an empty lot to remind us all of the folly of misguided friendships laid on a foundation of deceit, incompetence, and corruption.

To this day, I feel a tug of sadness and regret every time I pass the site, reminding me that I had grown up professionally in that wonderful institution, now replaced by a supermarket.

We now served only two hospitals. While Alex and DeeDee were assigned to the new acquisition, Koop, Butto, and I remained at our primary site. But because DeeDee was still not up to snuff in her surgical pathology skills and Alex was never that up-to-date in surgical pathology due to his other interests, surgical slides were quite often sent to Koop, Butto, and me for diagnoses, which became another source of complaint from us. I was asked repeatedly by Alex to make a daily trip to their hospital on my way to work to review their slides, but I refused because it was not on my way but rather quite out of my way.

The issue of Alex being away so frequently for his involvement with the College of American Pathologists (CAP) became a point of discontent, especially for Koop. Our weekly partnership meetings became quarrelsome and unpleasant, to say the least. We all gradually recognized the deterioration of our relationship, and so collectively, we decided to go on a retreat with a psychologist to sort out our feelings for each other. The only thing I remember about this trip was that during one of those awkward silences, I suggested a game of chess with Butto who actually sniffed his disapproval at playing the game of kings with me, someone who was obviously not up to his chess skills. So it was with some glee that I noted his shock when I won the game.

Despite this outing and our concerted efforts to keep our negative attitudes at bay, we continued on a downhill course. The final straw was when DeeDee decided to leave to be chief of a pathology department south of Boston. She did not invite us to be in on this as a group but was going to be the chief of pathology in a new hospital all by herself. The immediate consequence of this turn of event was that Alex needed someone to replace DeeDee. I volunteered because I knew that no one but I would work with Alex. Koop despised Alex while Butto disliked him no less. Neither of them, I felt, would miss me. I always felt that Koop tolerated me in a way he tolerated most women in general. It always amazed me to note how urbane his manners were toward DeeDee, whom I knew for a fact he couldn't stand. As for Butto, he regarded me as an older sister, someone who looked out for his interest and who had been a reliable conduit for his grievances to Henry and Alex until he became a full partner when he exercised his own voice, harshly at times.

Koop and Butto respected each other as pathologists.

One *thought* he was the best pathologist; the other *knew* he was the best pathologist. Very often during our surgical sign outs, the two men would pass slides to each other for consultation, totally ignoring my presence until I would remind them with "I'm here too, you know."

Relationship among the four of us was at a very low point. Once the decision was made that I would move, Koop regarded me as Alex's cohort, someone who could no longer be trusted. Once I decided to move, Alex started his campaign to convince me that we should break up the partnership. He and I would man the new hospital; Koop and Butto could take care of our home base.

Alex was right in his assessment that the partnership was doomed.

In fact, communication between the two groups ceased. The decision to break up our partnership was not an easy one for me to make. From my point of view, the advantages would all be in Alex's court. He would now gain a reliable, hardworking partner whose diagnostic skills he did not have to worry about, he would be able to continue with his CAP (College of American Pathologists) interest without interference, and he would no longer have to deal with Koop and Butto and their constant criticisms of his shortcomings.

I had by now worked with Alex for about twenty years. I had my own opinion about his weaknesses and strengths. At this stage, I frankly preferred him to Koop and Butto. I also happened to like him.

I eventually agreed with him to separate. We sold our private laboratory and agreed on some financial matters. We ceased contact and refused acknowledgement of their existence.

This was a terrible end for what we all hoped we would be a successful union. As I assumed my new position in a new hospital, I learned a religious group owned it. This was their flagship hospital where patients from their satellite facilities in neighboring states were sent for higher levels of care. It had less than two hundred beds and was not a teaching hospital. The strength of this institution rested on the will of this religious order to keep it alive and operating. Conversely, it was their greatest weakness too because they could close it any time they wanted.

The campus on which the hospital stood was situated in a woodsy area with a lovely pond facing the site. It also had a school, a chapel, and a new doctor's office building. My duties were not difficult, but it soon became evident that I could not handle everything with Alex's absence, which was frequent. So, we decided to employ one of our former residents, John, who had worked for us for a short period the year before. He was a very good pathologist and was free to take this opening at once. Together, we forged new relationships with the medical staff, particularly the surgeons who greatly appreciated our service.

When I first arrived at the hospital, I found the cryostat for our frozen section to be in such poor condition that I had to, on one occasion, go back to my razor blade method to render a diagnosis. The surgeon for whom I did the frozen section was so impressed that he personally went to the administration and demanded a new cryostat for our department, which we promptly received. Of course, this surgeon happened to bring in the largest number of patients to the hospital.

DeeDee claimed that she had tried for months to get the administration to replace the cryostat without any success.

A new hospital director was appointed soon after my arrival. He was a dentist who constantly assured the medical staff that he had plans A, B, C, and even D, to prevent any and all disasters that may befall the hospital. He lavished the staff with raffled gifts presented at our mundane medical meetings. Christmas parties were elaborate events held at the best restaurants in town with special chocolates worth hundreds of dollars placed on the diner's tables.

Soon, rumors swirled about the financial state of the hospital. Potential mergers were discussed and admitted to by the administration.

This progressed to potential buyers visiting the hospital, and when medical staff queried about these activities, we were repeatedly assured that the administration had backup plans A through D.

Approval was given to an assisted-living institution to be built on the campus, and that provided us with some degree of comfort and conviction that the hospital was not in dire straits. We carried out our professional tasks as usual on a particularly uneventful Friday.

But on Saturday, a surgeon called me to attend an emergency meeting at his home to discuss the hospital's possible bankruptcy. I was very surprised and astounded when I learned that it was not a possible bankruptcy but an actual bankruptcy. We were meeting to discuss what we could do as members of the medical staff to prevent this from happening. We decided that the entire medical staff would have to be called for a general meeting on Monday.

At this meeting, we were each asked to pledge an amount of money with our signatures to maintain the hospital until we could find a buyer. This amounted to a spectacular 1.3 million dollars pledged.

Next, we decided to invite the bondholder of the hospital to give us some insight into our financial problem, now that we had some cash to negotiate.

The bondsman came and listened politely to our plans of maintaining the hospital while we ferret out a buyer. He informed us that we were "burning" $100,000 a day, and our cash would last thirteen days. Did we think we could find a buyer within thirteen days?

It was obvious to all of us that the religious order had decided to abandon the hospital. Only they knew the reasons why.

The director landed softly in Maine in his golden parachute, and nine hundred employees lost their jobs in a blink of an eye. Plans A to D did not exist. They were all empty boasts from another deceitful and incompetent administrator. This hospital still stands empty while owners struggle with the local officials to convert it to condos.

Alex, John, and I were all out of a job. By now Alex had attained his goal of being at the top of the ladder at CAP. The years he spent there were fruitful for him and for all pathologists. He was instrumental in many ways in improving our professional lives, particularly his role in devising billing codes designed not to be detrimental to our incomes.

He had a summer place in New Hampshire and a medical license to practice there, so he thought he would do some per diem coverage for fellow pathologists in that area. I soon had an offer for a part-time job from a former resident who was now chief of three affiliated hospitals, the largest of which had over two hundred beds and that's where I would go.

With Alex's help, John also landed in the same place. Everyone in the department were young enough to be my children. Even though they treated me well with respect and even affection, I found it a difficult place to practice.

I had been blessed during my professional life to have had the two essential requirements that ensured a successful pathology practice: capable and reliable secretaries and histology technologists. With these twin necessities in place, checking each report carefully that I had to sign was not necessary. I did not have to worry whether the slides were cut to sufficient depth to show the abnormality nor did I need to spend time fussing with the proper staining qualities of the tissues on the slides. I had been so used to these amenities that I would sign my reports without reading them carefully and diagnose slides without wondering whether I was missing a deeper lesion or not.

These were not good habits to carry to a new hospital. During my first week there, I was visited by a surgeon who waved a report I had signed "normal placenta" on a man. When I asked the chief how something like this could happen, she placed her arm around me and said, "If you want something done right, you have to do it yourself."

I suddenly realized this was what everyone was doing on the computer at the end of the day— checking each surgical number to coincide with the patient and with the diagnosis and correcting all the wrong spelling, making sure that the secretaries did not make a fool out of them, as they did me.

The secretaries were the worst I had ever come across. They were unionized and were hard to dismiss. They absolutely did not care a hoot about the quality of their work. Tough for you if they erased or lost your dictation. And when that actually happened to me and they informed me that there was a backup copy somewhere in the bowels of the hospital, they showed not the slightest interest in retrieving it.

When they took a sick day, which they were entitled to do, they would choose to take it on the busiest day.

And why should they be careful in their typing or identifying the correct patient to type their reports on when they knew without a doubt that the pathologists spent hours checking everything they did every day anyway. What was odd to me was that no one complained much about them. Their sloppy and inefficient performance was accepted as a matter of course, perhaps because everyone feared their replacements might be even worse. At the start of my career, our secretaries could write letters on their own, responding to requests for slides or reports. When these secretaries were refused raises by the hospital due to salary caps on their grade levels, we paid them out of our own pockets because we valued them. At the end of my career, we were lucky to find secretaries who could spell.

Most hospitals spent approximately sixty percent of their budgets on salaries, so if they wanted to be profitable, they would need to shrink that portion of the expense. The only two ways one could do that would be to hire fewer people and/or to hire cheaper people. Successful managers often strived very hard to do both.

One possible way to save money in the general lab would be to employ techs who were versatile and could be rotated through different sections of the lab rather than pay more for techs with expertise only in one area, generalists instead of specialists. This would be most feasible in smaller labs with a limited menu of tests. But in well-managed larger labs, managers would be forced to deal with the different skill sets demanded in different areas such as in hematology, blood banking, and in microbiology, where cognitive skills are required, the lack of which could actually kill patients.

In histology, where techs cut tissues removed by surgery, special knowledge on how to position the tissue within paraffin blocks to cut it properly is essential. The tech would also need to know how deep to cut the tissue to show the complete lesion for diagnosis. If the cut was too superficial, no abnormality would be shown because the lesion would still be beneath the cut surface. If a lesion is extremely small, bad positioning could result in the entire lesion being cut "through" with no lesion left for diagnosis. A well-run high quality histology department is essential for the diagnostic accuracy of pathologists.

Although all the pathologists in the department were excellent, the support system for them was sorely missing.

The location of this particular histology department outside of the hospital added to the difficulties. No immediate consultation for any correction could take place. Any and all problems had to be relayed over the telephone, taking up precious time that neither side had.

The chief histologist in a middle-sized hospital like the one I was in would not be able to do the job well unless she was exceptionally well trained. Unfortunately, that appeared not to be the case. So, to compensate for possible deficiencies, rules upon rules were put into place to prevent disasters. For example, certain biopsies needed x number of sections to ensure the lesion would be present within the sections. This rule alone magnified the number of slides the pathologists had to review, not that we didn't have enough slides to diagnose each day.

The total number of surgical specimens for the three affiliated hospitals amounted to twenty-three thousand per year. This was handled by a total of six full-time pathologists and two part-timers in the two larger hospitals. The smallest hospital had no staff pathologist.

I aimed three times a week, which later was reduced to twice a week, because of economic reasons for the chief, to do as much as I could without leaving cases unsigned for someone else to follow up. This however was not always possible.

Despite my best effort to avoid blunders, I was involved in a case that needed the review of the quality-control committee. Although no further action was taken, this incident propelled me into being more on guard.

Any temporary relaxation of my unease was further dampened by an occurrence a week later. I had been examining a bone marrow section and even though there was nothing on the slide to indicate any abnormality, I detected a few strands of fibrous tissue present where I thought it shouldn't be. Intuitively, I asked for a deeper section and this revealed a metastatic cancer surrounded by dense reactive fibrous tissue.

The obvious implication here was, how many other cases have I not diagnose with lesions buried in paraffin blocks not sufficiently cut? I would break out in cold sweat just thinking about the possibility.

I thought about retiring, and in the twilight of my career, like a dying person remembering old journeys, I dredged up the images of former colleagues, tracing their footprints on the sands of our common pathway.

Dr. Dunham, who started me toward a career in pathology, lost his job a few years after I left to my former fellow resident Dan from the medical center. I ran into him once at a hospital where we were servicing the nuclear medicine department. I greeted him civilly but got back a mumbled reply. I did not see him again after that.

Henry, my boss for so many years, who nurtured and supported my struggles to be relevant during my nascent career, died peacefully in his sleep. So did my friend Humphrey in Canada.

Koop, who was so obsessed with the condition of his heart that he woefully neglected other parts of his body, discovered accidentally that he had a malignancy that had spread throughout his bones. He left work abruptly on the day of discovery and spent his last days with his wife on a farm, far, far away from the city they both loved, leaving Butto to be the sole member of our partnership to remain practicing at our "base" hospital.

Butto, whom I recruited, left me with a very bad taste in my mouth when we parted company. After a long period of silence between us, he suddenly appeared in my office one day and apologized to me for his behavior. I was very touched by his effort, and with tears in our eyes, we awkwardly made up. I have since visited him at our "base" hospital, chatting about old times and family.

Paul, the smartest surgeon on the North Shore, broke a lot of hearts among his supporters. He became a drunk, got thrown off the medical staff for outrageously neglecting his patients, almost set himself and his house on fire, sickened his surgical colleagues at the sight of him when he sought treatment in the ER, and died pitifully from his alcoholism.

Drs. Mann and Zack and Volker left this earth with enviable legacies.

Like the people passing through, the changing landscape in medicine also passed through my mind. When I was an intern, the patients I took care of were those without insurance and the hospital gave them free care. The passage of Medicare lifted the burden of hospitals and physicians in providing for the poor and uninsured but getting paid by the insurance for the insured was no piece of cake. Codes were devised for every diagnosis, and doctors had to hire teams of people to put in the right code for the right diagnosis and get it to the insurer within the specified period. I could never understand how anyone could use statistics from these coded diagnoses when doctors all coded to maximize payments. Not exactly lying as in lung cancer vs. pneumonia but definitely gastritis (if it paid more) vs. esophagitis (if it paid less). The gradual and increased stifling control of the insurance companies in the practice of medicine has resulted in large swaths of angry and frustrated doctors. The totally chaotic system of charges and payments for medical care that makes no sense coupled with the perennial pursuit of lowering payments to doctors, hospitals, and other healthcare entities impart at all times an atmosphere of siege everywhere. All these changes have produced a drop in the number of medical school applications by the best and the brightest of male candidates enabling a rise in the number of female students enrolled in medical schools. Although the steady increase in the number of female doctors may warm the hearts of feminist activists, I personally have a dreaded feeling that a predominance of female physicians will dim the traditional luster bestowed on the medical profession by the public. Already we are introduced today to nurse practitioners and physician assistants, entities that no patient can tell you what they are, except to give the impression that they are somewhat indistinguishable from doctors. Advertisements counsel "check with your pharmacists" with medical problems. Just one big common dumpster.

And what have I learned in the thirty-seven years in medicine?

I learned that the medical profession is a very tough one for women. To do well you either have to be single to devote all your energies to it or to be married to a very supportive husband. I was very lucky to have the latter. Our children were the first latchkey kids who came home an hour before Dad. He was the one who cooked an American meal (they didn't like Chinese) for them and a Chinese meal for us before I got back home. He was also the one who picked up the babysitter each morning and took her home each evening. He also took a year off when our sitter for the third child became unreliable, and we had used up all our vacation time filling the void.

I also learned that being a woman in a man's world had certain advantages but also special disadvantages. At social gatherings, when someone pointed me out as a pathologist, men would talk to me trying to gather some gory detail of my job while women would stay clearly away, intimidated by my M.D. degree. At professional meetings away from home, Alex would tell me what restaurants to go to, but my usual schedule was meeting to hotel room, to meeting to hotel room.

Between the mid-seventies until the mid-eighties, life was a total blur to me, filled with driving the kids to school, to piano lessons, to gymnastic lessons, to birthday parties, laced with my own frantic efforts in preparing for the various specialty examinations. Although the kids all did well in school, I watched over their progress anxiously and prodded them to do better by cajoling and bribing them. I struggled to teach them my views on keeping up with the Joneses when they complained bitterly that they were the only kids in school who did not have shirts with the little alligators. My oldest, who always had her own sense of style, had also expensive taste in clothing. Shopping for clothes became an unhappy experience because the desired item was always a little bit above the money we agreed we were going to spend. Since I did not want to continue to be unhappy or to cause unhappiness, I decided that I would give each child a sum of money each year to buy their own clothes excluding coats, shoes, and underwear. This was an instant success. I have never witnessed better shoppers in my life. To this day, they attribute their ability to handle money well to their clothing allowance. But my hectic life also had its funny moments. I remember when all three kids were in school, I agreed to feed them whatever they wanted each morning (in case they didn't eat the lunch at school) with the exception of bacon because of the grease. I told them they could have bacon on the weekends. As I went around taking orders one morning, I asked the youngest who was about five what she wanted. She said "eggs and bacon". After I patiently reminded her that she could only have that on the weekends, she looked at me seriously and said, "Okay, I'll just have fried chicken then."

Dr. E. Mei Shen

I did retire soon after. I was given a nice send-off party by the chief. Nice things were said about me, which elicited a reciprocal response.

Today, relieved of the burdens of diagnostic responsibilities, I luxuriate in a life of slow motion, reconnecting myself with my children on an adult level, helping to care for grandkids, and above all spending uninterrupted time improving my golf game with my husband and golfing friends.

All in all, it has been a wonderful journey.

About the Author

The author was born in Indonesia, then Dutch East Indies, because her father was a diplomat sent there by the Chinese government under Chiang Kai-shek. She grew up in different countries in Southeast Asia, receiving her medical degree while living in the Philippines. She came to the United States as an exchange student to further her postdoctoral training in Massachusetts. After a mandatory two-year exit from the United States due to visa requirement, she returned to the US in 1963 to begin her career in the practice of pathology.

Married over fifty years, she has three daughters, three grandsons and a granddaughter. She lives in Andover, Massachusetts, with her husband Joseph Hsieh.

www.ingramcontent.com/pod-product-compliance
Lightning Source LLC
LaVergne TN
LVHW091558060526
838200LV00036B/898